G Morel

Catalogue of a valuable collection of antique coins, comprising the Seleucid kings of Syria and autonomous and colonial coins of cities, collected in Syria

G Morel

Catalogue of a valuable collection of antique coins, comprising the Seleucid kings of Syria and autonomous and colonial coins of cities, collected in Syria

ISBN/EAN: 9783741163944

Manufactured in Europe, USA, Canada, Australia, Japa

Cover: Foto ©Andreas Hilbeck / pixelio.de

Manufactured and distributed by brebook publishing software (www.brebook.com)

G Morel

Catalogue of a valuable collection of antique coins, comprising the Seleucid kings of Syria and autonomous and colonial coins of cities, collected in Syria

CATALOGUE

OF

A VALUABLE COLLECTION OF

ANTIQUE COINS

COMPRISING

THE SELEUCID KINGS OF SYRIA

AND

AUTONOMOUS AND COLONIAL COINS OF CITIES

COLLECTED IN SYRIA

PRINTED BY

J. DAVY & SONS

DRYDEN PRESS, 137 LONG ACRE, LONDON

MDCCCLXXXVI

CATALOGUE

OF

A VALUABLE COLLECTION OF

ANTIQUE COINS

COMPRISING

THE SELEUCID KINGS OF SYRIA

AND

AUTONOMOUS AND COLONIAL COINS OF CITIES

Collected in Syria.

J. DAVY & SONS,
DRYDEN PRESS, 137, LONG ACRE, LONDON.

MDCCClxxxvi.

THE coins described in this catalogue have been collected during a residence of more than ten years at Beyrouth and in Lebanon, where the owner held an official appointment. The collection comprises coins of Syria and of the surrounding countries, such as the Seleucid Kings and autonomous as well as colonial coins of cities. Like every collection, it contains coins of ordinary interest, and others of rarity and value.

The series of the Seleucid Kings represents varieties and types of all the kings of the dynasty—specimens of which do not figure in many of the great European public collections. Most of the silver coins being in a good state of preservation, this collection may be regarded from an artistic as well as a scientific point of view; but the large number of copper coins, which are more valued by numismatists than by ordinary amateurs, give it also an important archæological value.

The series of the Imperial coins of Antioch, in silver and copper, is very extensive, and contains also rare and interesting specimens. Some of the Colonial sets of towns are equally worthy of attention.

It must be borne in mind that, although antique coins are an object of commerce, and can to a certain degree be procured in trade, it is not always that a tolerably complete collection of a certain series can be obtained ; and to form this is always a matter of time and of considerable expense. Indeed, certain coins cannot be bought at any price —and in order to obtain them amateurs have often had to wait year after year, until the death of some collector, who owned them, placed them possibly within their reach.

Although, as a rule, scientific numismatists do not attach a paramount importance to the state of preservation of antique coins, and consider them good when they are sufficiently clear to be an object of study ; such is not the case with amateurs—for them the value of a coin is increased in proportionto its degree of preservation and beauty.

In giving, therefore, in the following pages, a description of the coins, some pains have been taken to indicate, as clearly as possible, the condition they are in.

Very good stands for a coin which is perfect in every degree.

Good means that, although well preserved, it has circulated, and may be deficient in point of beauty, while conserving, nevertheless, all its archæological interest.

A coin marked *not good* must be understood to have suffered in some of its parts.

The system followed for classifying the Seleucid Kings is the one adopted in the catalogue of the British Museum, which has been reproduced for the description of many coins, and the plates referred to are those of that very valuable work.*

To indicate the *size* of the coins, the decimal system has been adopted. Thus 1· signifies that the size of the coin is 1 inch in diameter ; ·8=⅘ of an inch, &c. &c.

G. MOREL.

Note.—O = obverse. ℞ = reverse.

---

* " Catalogue of Greek Coins. The Seleucid Kings of Syria." by Percy Gardner, M.A. Edited by Reginald Stuart Poole. London, 1878.

THE SELEUCID KINGS OF SYRIA.

SELEUCUS I (NICATOR).

SILVER.

1 O· head of Heracles in lion's skin — ℞ ΣΕΛΕΥΚΟΥ
BAΣIΛΕΩΣ, Zeus seated to left holds eagle and sceptre ;
one monogram, below Δ I, *not very good*   *size* 1

2 O· similar—℞ same type and legend, before Zeus, small
head of Pallas ; under seat, star, *good*   *s.* 1·2½

3 O· similar—℞ same type and legend (drachma), *good s.* ·7

4 O· similar—℞ same legend, Zeus seated to left, holds
Nike, who presents to him wreath ; to left monogram,
below B E, *good*   *s.* 1·1

5 O· similar—℞ same type and legend ; two monograms,
good, but Nike rubbed out   *s.* 1·1

6 O· head of Zeus crowned with laurels—℞ BAΣIΛΕΩΣ
ΣΕΛΕΚΟΥ, four horned elephants harnessed to chariot,
in which stands Pallas fighting ; above, anchor before
Pallas, Σ, *very good*   *s.* 1

7 O· similar—℞ same type and legend, but no anchor,
medium   *s.* ·9

8 O· similar—℞ same type and legend (drachma)   *s.* ·7

9 O· tripod with cover—℞ BAΣIΛΕΩΣ ΣΕΛΕΚΟΥ, anchor
inverted (pierced) *good. Pl.* II, *No.* 2   *s.* ·3½

B

COPPER.

10 ○ head of Pallas, in Corinthian helmet—℞ ΒΑΣΙΛΕΩΣ
ΣΕΛΕΚΟΥ, Nike holding wreath and palm, crowns
name of Seleucus before her; *two coins, both good.*
Pl. II, *No.* 3

11 ○ heads of Dioscuri—℞ ΒΑΣΙΛΕΩΣ ΣΕΛ . . . Elephant's
head, to right M, *medium. Pl.* II, *No.* 10

12 ○ head of Apollo to right, laurelled—℞ ΒΑΣΙΛΕΩΣ
ΣΕΛΕΚΟΥ, Athene Akis to right; *three coins, all good.*
Pl. II, *No.* 13

13 ○ head of Medusa to right, winged—℞ ΒΑΣΙΛΕΩΣ
ΣΕΛΕΚΟΥ, Indian bull to right butting ; *three coins*
₊ Sizes ·9 above Θ, ·8 below Ξ, ·5, all good. *Pl.* II, *No.* 14

14 ○ head of Apollo with long hair laurelled— ℞ ΒΑΣΙΛΕΩΣ
ΣΕΛΕΚΟΥ, tripod with round cover, *good. Pl.* II, *No.* 16

COPPER COINS, PROBABLY STRUCK BY SELEUCUS I,
Not in Catalogue British Museum.

15 ○ head of Apollo, full face—℞ ΒΑΣΙΛΕΩΣ ΣΕΛΕΚΟΥ,
elephant to left, curved on obverse side ; has the
appearance of copper coins struck in Mesopotamia,
medium   *s.* 1·05

16 ○ head of man, bearded and laurelled — ℞ ΒΑΣ
[ΙΛΕΩΣ Σ]ΕΛΕΚ[ΟΥ], man driving quadrige of
horses, *not very good*   *s.* ·8

17 ○ head of man with horns, full face—℞ ΒΑΣΙΛΕΩΣ
ΣΕΛΕΚΟΥ, horse to right   *s.* ·6½

18 ○ head of Heracles in lion's skin—℞ no legend, anchor
and various implements   *s.* 5½

ANTIOCHUS I (SOTER).

SILVER.

19 ○ young head of Antiochus to right in border of dots—
℞ ΒΑΣΙΛΕΩΣ ΑΝΤΙΟΧΟΥ, Apollo seated to left on
Omphalos, holds bow and two arrows ; two monograms,
○ *medium,* ℞ *very good. Pl.* III, *No.* 3.   *s.* 1·1

20 O· middle-aged head of Antiochus, diad. to right—
Ŗ· same legend, Apollo seated on omphalos, holds bow
and arrow; two monograms, *good. Pl.* III, *No.* 4 *s.* 1·2

21 O· similar ; circle of dots around head and reverse—
Ŗ· same type and legend ; two monograms, *good s.* 1·2

COPPER.

22 O· young head of Antiochus, diad. to right—Ŗ· ΒΑΣΙΛΕΩΣ
ΑΝΤΙΟΧΟΥ, Nike to right, holds wreath over inverted
anchor, *good. Pl.* IV, *No.* 1, *but smaller* *s.* ·6

23 O· Macedonian shield ; on the boss, anchor—Ŗ· same
legend, horned elephant to right, above ME and club,
very good. Pl. IV, *No.* 7 *s.* ·8

24 O· similar—Ŗ· similar; above elephant, monogram and
anchor, *medium*

25 O· head of Zeus to right, laurelled—Ŗ· same inscription,
thunderbolt, above club; below jaw-bone of boar,
good *s.* ·8

26 O· head of Apollo, three-quarter face, to left laurelled—Ŗ·
same inscription, Nike erecting trophy, *medium* *s* ·6

27 O· head of Apollo laurelled—Ŗ· same inscription, Apollo
seated on omphalos, holds arrow, left arm rests on
lyre, *good* *s.* ·6

28 O· beardless head of Zeus (or Apollo ?)—Ŗ· same inscription, tripod with cover ; *three coins, all good s.* ·6 *to* ·7
⁎⁎ Size, 1° counter mark, anchor ; 2° to left, monogram
3° below, anchor.

29 O· elderly head of Antiochus, right diadem—Ŗ· same inscription, Apollo seated on omphalos, holds bow and
arrow ; *three coins, good. Pl.* 10, *No.* 4 *s.* ·5½, ·3, ·7

ANTIOCHUS II (THEOS).

SILVER.

30 O· head of Antiochus, right diadem with circle of dots—
Ŗ· ΒΑΣΙΛΕΩΣ ΑΝΤΙΟΧΟΥ, Heracles bearded, seated
to left on rocks, holds in right club, left rests on rocks,
lion's skin round loins ; to left vase and monogram,
very good. Pl. V, *No.* 6 *s.* 1·15

4

SELEUCUS II (Callinicus).

SILVER.

31 O head of Seleucus with small whiskers, diadem—℞ ΒΑΣΙΛΕΩΣ ΣΕΛΕΚΟΥ, Apollo naked, standing, holds bow and arrow and leans on tripod ; to left two monograms, *good* s. 1·15

32 O similar—℞ similar, to left monogram, to right N, *good* s. 1·15

COPPER.

33 O head of Seleucus—℞ same inscription, horse trotting to left, above stars of Dioscuri, between horse's legs, monogram, *medium. Pl.* VI, *No.* 5 s. ·6

34 O head of Pallas in helmet—℞ same inscription, Apollo naked standing, holds bow and arrow, *good. Pl.* VI, *No.* 6 s. ·6

35 O head of Seleucus bearded—℞ same inscription, Pegasus galloping to left, *medium. Pl.* VI, *No.* 16 s. ·6

36 O head of Apollo—℞ same inscription, bull walking. *Pl.* VI, *No.* 12 s. ·6

ANTIOCHUS (Hierax).

SILVER.

37 O head of Antiochus, right, diademed—℞ ΒΑΣΙΛΕΩΣ ΑΝΤΙΟΧΟΥ, Apollo seated on omphalos, holds bow and arrow, to left ΛΕ ; to right ΔΙ, type represented *Pl.* VII, *No.* 2, *very good* s. 1·1

COPPER.

38 O head of Antiochus—℞ same inscription, draped female (Minerva ?) full face, holding in left hand small figure of Victory, *good* s. ·9

39 O same head—℞ same inscription, Nike holding long palm in right, *medium. Pl.* VII, *No.* 5 s. ·7½

UNDETERMINED COINS OF FIRST ANTIOCHII,
Not contained in Catalogue British Museum.

COPPER.

40 O elephant going to right—℞ ΒΑΣΙΛΕΩΣ ΑΝΤΙΟΧΟΥ, winged figure of Victory to right ; *two coins, not very good* *s.* '9, ·6
41 O head of king to right—℞ same inscription, horse trotting to right (very thick), *medium* *s.* ·6
42 O head of king in helmet to right—℞ same inscription. prow of galley to right, *good* *s.* ·5½
43 O young head of male deity to right—℞ same inscription (in very small letters) ; winged figure carrying long palm on her shoulder to right, *medium* *s.* ·8½
44 O head of bearded king in helmet to right in circle of dots—℞ ΒΑΣΙΛΕΩΣ ΑΝΤΙΟΧΟΥ, Demeter seated to left, leaning on shield, holds in hand small figure ; the whole in circle of dots, *medium* *s.* 9½

⁎ Very thick coin, bought in Lebanon, but does not seem to be of Syrian origin.

SELEUCUS III (CERAUNUS).

SILVER.

45 O head of Seleucus, right diademed—℞ ΒΑΣΙΛΕΩΣ ΣΕΛΕΚΟΥ, Apollo seated on omphalos to left, holds bow and arrow to left, monogram to right ; monogram, *medium*. *Pl.* VII, *No.* 6 *s.* 1·1½
46 O the same—℞ similar, to right monogram, *good* *s.* 1·1½

COPPER.

47 O head of Artemis, hair bound with fillet—℞ ΒΑΣΙΛΕΩΣ ΣΕΛΕΚΟΥ, Apollo seated on omphalos, holds bow and arrow ; *eight coins, mostly good. Pl.* VII, *No.* 10 *s.* ·5 *to* ·6

ANTIOCHUS III (THE GREAT).

SILVER.

48 O head of Antiochus, young, in fillet border — ℞ ΒΑΣΙΛΕΩΣ ΑΝΤΙΟΧΟΥ, Apollo seated on omphalos, holds bow and arrow ; to left monogram, *good* *s.* 1·1

49 ☉ the same—℞ similar; to right monogram, *good* s. 1·05
50 ☉ head of Antiochus old, in fillet border—℞ similar; no monogram, *very good* s. 1·2
51 ☉ the same—℞ similar, *very good* s. 1·2
52 ☉ the same—℞ similar; to left monogram, to right ΔΙ, *very good* s. 1·2
53 ☉ the same—℞ similar; monogram rubbed out, *medium*, s. 1·2
54 ☉ the same, in border of dots—℞ similar; to left monogram, *good* s. 1·1½
55 ☉ the same, young face—℞ similar; to left A, *good* s. ·7½ *drachma*

COPPER.

56 ☉ head of Antiochus—℞ ΒΑΣΙΛΕΩΣ ΑΝΤΙΟΧΟΥ, hinder part of galley with rudder; date ΡΚΔ (124), *good. Pl.* ix, *No.* 3
57 ☉ the same—℞ same inscription; elephant to right, driver seated on neck behind tripod, *medium. Pl.* ix, *No.* 5 s. ·7
58 ☉ the same—℞ same inscription, forepart of galley, no date; *two coins—one good, one medium*
59 ☉ the same—℞ same inscription, Nike to left holding wreath; to left monogram and horse's head, to right monogram, *good. Pl.* ix, *No.* 6 s. ·1
60 ☉ the same—℞ same inscription, palm-tree. *Pl.* ix, *No.* ·8 (Tyre) s. ·5½
61 ☉ the same—℞ same inscription, Apollo naked, standing, holds bow and arrow. *Pl.* ix, *No.* 11 s. ·4½

SELEUCUS IV (Philopater).

SILVER.

62 ☉ head of Seleucus, right, diademed—℞ ΒΑΣΙΛΕΩΣ ΣΕΛΕΚΟΥ, Apollo seated on omphalos, holds bow and arrow, fillet border; to left palm and wreath, in exergue monogram, *good. Pl.* 10, *No.* 5 s. ·1½
63 ☉ the same—℞ similar; to left aplustre, below monogram, *good* s. 1·½

COPPER.

64 ☉ head of Seleucus—℞ ΒΑΣΙΛΕΩΣ ΣΕΛΕΚΟΥ, hinder
part of galley with rudder ; date ΡΑΙ   *s.* ·8½
Not in Catalogue British Museum.

65 ☉ head of Apollo, behind monogram—℞ same inscription, Apollo standing naked rests on tripod ; serrated
edge, *good. Pl.* x, *No.* 9   *s.* ·9⅓

66 ☉ the same—℞ similar, *good*   *s.* ·9

67 ☉ the same—℞ similar, *medium*   *s.* ·8

68 ☉ bust of Dionysius—℞ same inscription, forepart of
galley : above monogram, *medium. Pl.* x, *No.* 12 *s.* ·8

69 ☉ bust of Artemis—℞ same inscription, Artemis standing, holds spear ; behind her roe, *medium. Pl.* x, *No.* 11
      s. ·7

70 ☉ same—℞ similar, *good*   *s.* ·7

ANTIOCHUS IV. (Epiphanes).

SILVER.

71 ☉ head of Antiochus with diadem, fillet border—℞
ΒΑΣΙΛΕΩΣ ΑΝΤΙΟΧΟΥ ΘΕΟΥ ΕΠΙΦΑΝΟΥΣ, Zeus
seated on throne, holds Nike to right, rests on sceptre ;
in ex. monogram, *very good. Pl.* xi, *No.* 8   *s.* 1·3

72 ☉ the same—℞ same inscription, and in ex. ΝΙΚΗΦΟΡΟΥ,
Zeus, seated as above, with himation over shoulder,
holds Nike to left ; to left monogram, *medium*   *s.* 1·3

73 ☉ the same—℞ similar, to left monogram (head rubbed
in cleaning), *reverse good*   *s.* 1·2

74 ☉ head of Antiochus, diadem to right in border of dots—
℞ ΒΑΣΙΛΕΩΣ ΑΝΤΙΟΧΟΥ ΕΠΙΦΑΝΟΥΣ, Apollo
seated on omphalos holds bow and arrow ; in ex. Ο,
very good. Pl. xi, *No.* 4   *s.* ·7

75 ☉ the same—℞ similar, *good*   *s.* ·7

76 ☉ the same—℞ same inscription, tripod lebes ; to left
monogram and Γ, *very good*   *s.* ·7

77 ☉ the same—℞ same inscription, winged figure of
Victory to left, holding wreath in extended arm, *good*
      s. ·5¼

COPPER.

78 ℺ head of Antiochus to right radiate—℞ ΒΑΣΙΛΕΩΣ
ΑΝΤΙΟΧΟΥ, Kybele seated on throne to left holds
Nike, at her feet bird, under seat two dots, *good.*
Pl. xii, *No.* 2   *s.* ·8

79 ℺ similar—℞ the same, *good*   *s.* 1·2¼

80 ℺ the same—℞ same inscription (indistinct) Zeus seated
on throne, *not good. Type Pl.* xii, *No.* 5   *s.* ·6

81 ℺ same head — ℞ ΒΑΣΙΛΕΩΣ ΑΝΤΙΟΧΟΥ ΘΕΟΥ
ΕΠΙΦΑΝΟΥΣ, Zeus standing, holds thunderbolt ; *two
coins, good*   *s.* ·7 *and* ·6¼

82 ℺ same head—℞ same inscription, Ægis, *medium. Pl.* xii,
No. 7   *s.* ·7

83 ℺ same head—℞ same inscription, Zeus standing, at his
feet bird, *good. Pl.* xii, *No.* 6   *s.* ·8

84 ℺ same head—℞ ΒΑΣΙΛΕΩΣ ΑΝΤΙΟΧΟΥ, female figure
facing, holding in right long sceptre, serrated edge ;
two coins, good. Pl. xii, *No.* 10   *s.* ·55

85 ℺ head of Zeus Serapis—℞ ΒΑΣΙΛΕΩΣ ΑΝΤΙΟΧΟΥ
ΘΕΟΥ ΕΠΙΦΑΝΟΥΣ, eagle with closed wings to right
standing on thunderbolt ; *two coins, good. Pl.* xii,
No. 11   *s.* 1·3

86 ℺ Bust of Isis—℞ same inscription, eagle as above ; *two
coins, good. Pl.* xii, *No.* 12   *s.* 3

87 ℺ head of Antiochus radiate—℞ similar inscription, eagle
as above, but turned to left ; *six coins, medium. Type
of Pl.* xii, *No.* 10   *s.* ·65

88 ℺ head of Antiochus radiate, ΒΑΣΙΛΕΩΣ ΑΝΤΙΟΧΟΥ—
℞ ΣΙΔΟΝΙΩΝ, with Phenician inscription, Europa
seated on bull galloping to left, holds bull's horns and
end of veil ; *two coins, good. Sidon, Pl.* xii, *No.* 15, *s.* ·7

89 ℺ head of Antiochus — ℞ ΒΑΣΙΛΕΩΣ ΑΝΤΙΟΧΟΥ
ΤΥΡΙΩΝ, Phenician inscription, galley, *not good. Tyre*
                                                     s. ·8

90 ℺ same head—℞ ΒΑΣΙΛΕΩΣ ΑΝΤΙΟΧΟΥ, with Phenician
inscription, Poseidon facing, holds patera and trident ;
to left monogram, *medium. Laodicea, Pl.* xii, *No.* 16
                                                     s. ·8

91 ☧ same head—℞ ΑΝΤΙΟΧΕΩΝ ΤΩΝ ΠΡΟΣ ΔΑΦΝΗΙ, Zeus facing, head to left, holds wreath in outstretched arm ; to left monogram, to right monogram, *very good. Antiochea ad Daphnen, Pl.* xiii, *No.* 1   *s.* ·8

92 ☧ same head—℞ similar to left, monogram to right, AB, *good*

93 ☧ same head—℞ similar, to left monogram, to right AB, in ex. ΔΜΡ, *very good*

94 ☧ same head—℞ ΣΕΛΕΚΕΩΝΤΩΝ ΤΩΝ ΕΜΠΙΕΡΑΙ, winged thunderbolt, *medium. Seleucia in Syria, Pl.* xiii, *No.* 6   *s.* ·9

95 ☧ same head—℞ similar, *very good*   *s.* ·9

COPPER COINS OF ANTIOCHUS EPIPHANES,

Not in Catalogue of British Museum.

96 ☧ head of Antiochus to left radiate—℞ ΒΑΣΙΛΕΩΣ ΑΝΤΙΟΧΟΥ, Winged Victory in biga of horses to left, below monogram, *good*   *s.* ·7

97 ☧ jugated heads of Antiochus and Queen--℞ ΤΡΙΠΟΛΙ- ΤΩΝ, Dioscuri on horseback to right, below date ΞΜΡ, *good*   *s.* ·7

98 ☧ head of Antiochus radiate, ΒΑΣΙΛΕΩΣ ΑΝΤΙΟΧΟΥ—℞ male figure of Kronos as represented upon autonomous coins of Byblos, below Phenician inscription. Byblos ? *distinct but not good*   *s.* ·8

99 ☧ head of Antiochus in middle of shield—℞ ΑΛΕΞΑΝ- ΔΡΕΩΝ, Zeus standing, as represented upon coins of Antiochea ad Daphnen ; *very thick coin, good*   *s.* ·8

ANTIOCHUS IV OR V.

COPPER WITH SERRATED EDGE.

100 ☧ bust of Demeter veiled—℞ ΒΑΣΙΛΕΩΣ ΑΝΤΙΟΧΟΥ, elephant's head to left ; *two coins, good. Pl.* xiii, *No.* 9   *s.* ·5 *to* ·6

101 O head of Apollo to right laurelled—℞ same inscription, Apollo seated on omphalos, holds bow and arrow,
to left aplustre ; *very good, four coins.* *Pl.* XIII, *No.* 10
s. ·5 *to* ·6
102 O the same, behind monogram—℞ the same, *very good*

ANTIOCHUS V (EUPATOR).

SILVER.

103 O head of Antiochus to right in fillet border—℞
ΒΑΣΙΛΕΩΣ ΑΝΤΙΟΧΟΥ. ΕΥΠΑΤΟΡΟΣ, Zeus seated
to left, holds Nike who crowns king's name ; rests on
sceptre, to left ΔI, *very good.* *Pl.* XIII, *No.* 14 *s.* 1·1
104 O the same—℞ same inscription and type ; to left monogram of Ptolémaïs, *good.* *Pl.* XIII, *No.* 12 *s.* 1·2
105 O the same—℞ similar, to left monogram, *medium s.* 1·2
106 O head of Antiochus to right in border of dots, behind
monogram—℞ ΒΑΣΙΛΕΩΣ ΑΝΤΙΟΧΟΥ ΕΥΠΑΤΟ-
ΡΟΣ, eagle to left on thunderbolt ; to left palm ; be
tween eagle's legs monogram, the whole in border of
dots *s.* 1·2
*** Plated, the silver being worn out in sundry places.
Not in catalogue British Museum. See in "Monnaies
datées des Séleucides," by M. de Saulcy, *p.* 27, the
remarks made by the author about a silver tetra-
drachme of the same type,—probably the only one
known in Mr. Peretié's collection at Beyrouth.

DEMETRIUS I (SOTER).

SILVER.

107 O head of Demetrius in border of dots—℞ ΒΑΣΙΛΕΩΣ
ΔΗΜΗΤΡΙΟΥ ΣΩΤ . . . Apollo seated on omphalos
(drachma), *not very good.* *Pl.* XIV, *No.* 5 *s.* ·6
108 O head of Demetrius to right, diademed border of laurel
wreath—℞ ΒΑΣΙΛΕΩΣ ΔΗΜΗΤΡΙΟΥ ΣΩΤΗΡΟΣ,
Tyche or Demeter seated on throne, supported by
winged female monster ; holds sceptre and cornucopia,
to left monogram, date ΞΡ, *very good* *s,* 1·2

109 O- same head—℞ similar, to left monogram, date HNP, *good* s. 1·25
110 O- same head—℞ ΒΑΣΙΛΕΩΣ ΔΗΜΗΤΡΙΟΥ, Demeter seated as above, *very good* s. 1·15
111 O- same head—℞ similar, to left monogram, *good* s. 1·2
112 O- same head—℞ similar, to left monogram (Heraclea), *good* s. 1·2
113 O- same head, fillet border—℞ ΒΑΣΙΛΕΩΣ ΔΗΜΗΤΡΙΟΥ ΣΩΤΗΡΟΣ, cornucopia, monograms (Antioch) date ΞΡ, *very good* s. ·75
114 O- same head—℞ similar, monograms, date ΛΞΡ, *not good* s. ·7

COPPER.

115 O- head of Demetrius—℞ ΒΑΣΙΛΕΩΣ ΔΗΜΗΤΡΙΟΥ ΤΥΡΙΩΝ, and Phenician inscription, part of galley, date HNP, *Tyre, good* s. ·8
116 O- same heads—℞ similar, but dates and Phenician inscription not clear; *two coins*
117 O- same head—℞ similar, but no Phenician inscription; *two coins, good*
118 O- same head—℞ similar, date HNP, *good* s. ·8
119 O- same head—℞ similar, date ΘΝΡ; *two coins, good*
120 O- same head behind ΜΙ—℞ ΒΑΣΙΛΕΩΣ ΔΗΜΗΤΡΙΟΥ ΣΙΔΩΝΙΩΝ and Phenician inscription. *Sidon, two coins, good* s. ·75

ALEXANDER BALA.

SILVER.

121 O- head of Alexander to right, diadem in border of dots —ΑΛΕΞΑΝΔΡΟΥ ΒΑΣΙΛΕΩΣ, eagle with closed wings standing on beak of galley, over shoulder palm; to left monogram of Tyre, to right monogram date ΕΞΡ, *Tyre, good* s. 1
122 O- same head—℞ same inscription but title of ΒΑΣΙΛΕΩΣ left out in striking; same type but eagle standing on palm, date ΓΞΡ to left, monogram, to right trident, *fleur de coin. Berytus* s. 1·1

123 ○ same head—℞ same inscription, eagle with palm over shoulder, to right ΣΙΔΩ, and aplustre, date ΓΞΡ. *good. Sidon* *s.* 1

124 ○ same head in fillet border—℞ ΒΑΣΙΛΕΩΣ ΑΛΕΞΑΝ· ΔΡΟΥ ΘΕΟΠΑΤΟΡΟΣ ΕΥΕΡΓΕΤΟΥ, Zeus seated on throne holds Nike and sceptre ; below Δ, *medium s.* 1·15

125 ○ same head—℞ similar, below monogram, *medium. Heraclea* *s.* 1·3

126 ○ same head—℞ similar, below monogram and date ΕΞΡ, *medium* *s.* 1·2

127 ○ same head in border of dots—℞ same inscription Apollo seated on Omphalos to right, *good* *s.* ·85

⁎ Not in catalogue of British Museum. Very thick and fine didrachm of great rarity.

128 ○ same head—℞ same inscription, Apollo seated on Omphalos, below monogram, *good. Heraclea ; drachma* *s.* ·7

129 ○ same head—℞ similar, with no monograms, *good, drachmas two coins* *s.* ·7

130 ○ same head in fillet border—ΒΑΣΙΛΕΩΣ ΑΛΕΞΑΝ· ΔΡΟΥ ΘΕΟΠΑΤΟΡΟΣ ΕΥΕΡΓΕΤΟΥ, Zeus seated holding Nike, *very good* *s.* 1·15

COPPER.

131 ○ head of Alexander to right, diad.—℞ ΒΑΣΙΛΕΩΣ ΑΛΕΞΑΝΔΡΟΥ, Zeus seated on throne holds Nike and sceptre, throne rests on anchor, serrated edge, *medium. Pl.* xvi, *No.* 5 *s.* ·8

132 ○ same head—℞ same inscription, Pallas armed holds Nike, in left hand spear and shield, serrated edge ; to left monogram (*Heraclea*) in exergue monogram, *good· Pl.* xvi, *No.* 7 *s.* ·8

133 ○ head of Alexander in lion's skin—℞ same inscription, Apollo naked, standing, holds bow and arrow ; *two coins, one good and one medium. Pl.* xvi, *No.* 10 *s.* ·8

134 ○ head of Alexander, wearing crested helmet—℞ same inscription, Nike holds palm and crowns, name of Alexander, to left ear of corn ; *three coins, two good and one medium. Pl.* xvi, *No.* 11 *s.* ·7

135　O head of Alexander—℞ ΛΝΤΙΟΧΕΩΝ, Zeus facing, head turned to left, date ΓΞΡ, *Antioch, medium. Pl. xvii, No.* 1　　　　　　　　*s.* ·85

136　O same head — ℞ ΑΠΑΜΕΩΝ, Zeus standing to left, *Apameo, not good. Pl.* xvii, *No.* 2　　　*s.* ·85

COPPER COINS OF ALEXANDER BALA,
Not in Catalogue of British Museum.

137　O head of Alexander covered with lion's skin (counter-marked with scorpion)—℞ ΛΛΕΞΛΝΔΡΕ(ΩΝ), Zeus standing to left, arm extended ; to left two monograms, *good*　　　　　　　　　　　*s.* ·75

138　O head of Alexander to right—℞ ΒΑΣΙΛΕΩΣ ΛΛΕΞΑΝ-ΔΡΟΥ, and Phenician inscription, Poseidon standing and facing holds patera and trident ; to left ΛΑ, to right monogram (*Laodicea*), *good*　　　　*s.* ·8

139　O head of Alexander—℞ ΒΑΣΙΛΕΩΣ ΛΛΕΞΑΝΔΡΟΥ, galley, serrated edge ; *two coins, good*　　*s.* ·6

140　O head of Alexander—℞ legend indistinct, palm tree, *not good*　　　　　　　　　　　*s.* ·55

141　O ΒΑΣΙΛΕΩC ΛΛΕΞΑΝΔΡΟC around anchor — ℞ Wheel, between the spokes Hebrew letters, *not distinct*　　　　　　　　　　　　　　*s.* ·6

142　O head of Alexander—℞ ΣΕΛΕΥΚΕΩΝ . . . . . thunder-bolt in crown of leaves, *medium*　　　　*s.* ·9

DEMETRIUS II.

SILVER.

143　O head of Demetrius, diad., border of dots—℞ ΔΗΜΗ-ΤΡΙΟΥ ΒΑΣΙΛΕΩΣ, eagle to left, with palm over shoulder ; to right monogram and date OP, to right ΣΙΔ and aplustre, *good. Sidon, Pl.* xvii, *No.* 7　s. 1

144　O head of Demetrius in fillet border—℞ ΒΑΣΙΛΕΩΣ ΔΗΜΗΤΡΙΟΥ ΘΕΟΥ ΦΙΛΑΔΕΛΦΟΥ ΝΙΚΑΤΟΡΟΣ, Apollo seated on omphalos holds bow and arrow　H, in ex. date ΗΞΡ, *good. Pl.* xvii, *No.* 8　　s. 1.1

14

145 O same head—℞ same inscription, Tyche seated to
left on throne, holds sceptre and cornucopia, *good*.
Pl. xviii, *No.* 2   *s.* '1

COPPER.

146 O head of Demetrius to right diad.—℞ same inscription, Artemis standing to right, in ex. date ΘΞP.
medium. Pl. xviii, *No.* 5   *s.* '1

147 O Head of Zeus to right laureate—℞ same inscription,
Apollo seated on omphalos with bow and arrow, *good*.
Pl. xviii, *No.* 11   *s.* '9

148 O head of Zeus to right laureate—℞ same inscription,
winged Pallas to left, holds Nike, shield and spear,
good. Pl. xviii, *No.* 12   *s.* '95

149 O head of Apollo—℞ same inscription, tripod lebes, in
ex. two monograms, *very good. Antioch, Pl.* xviii,
No. 14   *s.* '75

ANTIOCHUS VI (Dionysus).

SILVER.

150 O head of Antiochus radiate, fillet border—℞ ΒΑΣΙΛΕΩΣ
ΑΝΤΙΟΧΟΥ ΕΠΙΦΑΝΟΥΣ ΔΙΟΝΙΣΟΥ, the Dioscuri
on horseback to left, lance couched, within wreath ; to
left, date OP ; to right, three monograms, *good. Pl.*
xix, *No.* 2   *s.* 1·3

151 O same head—℞ similar, *good*   *s.* 1·25

152 O same head—℞ similar date OΞP, to right I Π K, *not
good*   *s.* 1·15

153 O same head in border of dots—℞ same inscription,
Apollo seated on omphalos, holds bow and arrow,
date OP, between legs monogram, and ΣTA (drachma),
very good. Pl. xix, *No.* 3   *s.* '7

154 O same head—℞ same inscription and type (drachma),
not good

155 O same head in fillet border—℞ same inscription,
Macedonian helmet, above TPY (drachma), *pierced,
and not good. Pl.* xix, *No.* 7   *s.* '7

COPPER.

156 O head of Antiochus, radiate—℞ same inscription, Amphora, to left monogram, *good. Pl.* XIX, *No.* 9 *s.* ·85

157 O same head—℞ same inscription and type, no monogram; *two coins, medium* *s.* ·85

158 O head of Antiochus as Dionysus, radiate, ivy crowned —℞ same inscription, elephant to left, holding torch in trunk, to right ΣΤΑ and star, serrated edge; *three coins, very good. Pl.* XIX, *No.* 12 *s.* ·8 *to* ·9

159 O head of Antiochus, radiate — ℞ same inscription, panther to left, holding palm with mouth and forepaw, serrated edge, above ΣΤΑ to right palm; *three coins, very good. Pl.* XIX, *No.* 14 *s.* ·7

160 O head of Antiochus, radiate — ℞ same inscription, Dionysos to left, clad in chiton and clothurni, leans on spear, and holds inclined vase in right hand, type similar to *Pl.* XIX, *No.* 8, but larger and better, *very good* *s.* ·95

TRYPHON.

SILVER.

161 O head of Tryphon—℞ ΒΑΣΙΛΕΩΣ ΤΡΥΦΩΝΟΣ ΑΥΤΟΚΡ . . . . ΡΟΣ, eagle on thunderbolt to left, to left monogram, to right L. Δ., the head, legend and monograms are distinct and legible, but the coin is in very bad condition, having been rubbed on both sides for cleaning *s.* 1·1

162 O head of Tryphon, diadem—℞ same inscription, Macedonian helmet, to left monogram (drachma), *good. Pl.* XX, *No.* 2 *s.* ·7

COPPER.

163 O head of Tryphon to right, diadem—℞ same inscription, spiked helmet, to left Α. Σ. and ΑΣΚ (Ascalon), *three coins, very good* *s.* ·7

164 O the same—℞ similar, to left palm, *good*

165 O the same—℞ similar, to left Pilei of Dioscuri, *good*

166 O the same—℞ similar, no monogram, *good*

ANTIOCHUS VII (SIDETES).

SILVER.

167 ○ bust of Antiochus to right, diadem, in border of dots
—℞ ΑΝΤΙΟΧΟΥ ΒΑΣΙΛΕΩΣ, eagle with closed wings
to left, over shoulder palm, to left date ΕΟΡ and
monogram, to right ΣΙΔΩ, and aplustre (Sidon), *good*.
Pl. xx, *No.* 4   *s.* 1·15

168 ○ same bust—℞ same inscription, eagle on beak of
galley, to left monogram, and monogram on club, to
right ΑΣ and date ΔΟΡ (Tyre), *good*   *s.* 1·1

169 ○ same bust—℞ similar, date ΕΟΡ, *good*   *s.* 1·1

170 ○ same bust—℞ similar, date ΖΟΡ, *very good*   *s.* 1·1

171 ○ same bust—℞ similar, *good*   *s.* 1·1

172 ○ same bust—℞ similar, date ΕΟΡ (didrachm); *two
coins, good*   *s.* ·85

173 ○ head of Antiochus to right—℞ ΒΑΣΙΛΕΩΣ ΑΝΤΙΟΧΟΥ
ΕΥΕΡΓΕΤΟΥ, Pallas armed, standing to left, holds
Nike, the whole in wreath of laurel, to left monogram
of Tyre on club, and ΙΕΡ ΑΣΥ   *s.* 1·15
⁎ Lower part of face spoilt by cleaning, reverse very good.

174 ○ head of Antiochus to right, diademed, in fillet border
—℞ ΒΑΣΙΛΕΩΣ ΑΝΤΙΟΧΟΥ ΕΥΕΡΓΕΤΟΥ, Pallas
armed, standing to left, holding Nike, in laurel wreath,
to left monogram, to right ΑΙ, *very good*   *s.* 1·25

175 ○ same head—℞ same inscription and type, to left
monogram, to right monogram, *very good*

176 ○ same head—℞ similar, to left monogram, *good* *s.* 1·2

177 ○ same head—℞ similar, to left monogram, to right
monogram, *good*   *s.* 1·2

COPPER.

178 ○ bust of Eros—℞ same inscription, head dress of Isis,
date ΕΟΡ, below aplustre, *very good*. *Pl.* xx, *No.* 11
                                                                          s. ·7

179 ○ the same—℞ similar date, ΕΠΡ; two other similar
coins, dates illegible, *medium*

Copper Coins of Antiochus VII,
Not in collection British Museum.

180 O head of Antiochus to right—℞ ΒΑΣΙΛΕΩΣ ΑΝΤΙΟΧΟΥ, galley, above ΙΕΡΑΣ ΑΣΥ, date ΞΟΡ, below ΤΥΡΙΩΝ, and Phenician letters; *two coins, one good, and one inferior* s. ·9

181 O same head—℞ same inscription and type, date ΘΟΡ, and Phenician letters, *good* s. ·8

DEMETRIUS II NICATOR (Restored).

SILVER.

182 O bust of Demetrius without beard, wearing chlamis, diademed—℞ ΔΗΜΗΤΡΙΟΥ ΒΑΣΙΛΕΩΣ, eagle with closed wings, standing on back of galley, with palm over shoulder, to left monogram, and monogram on club, to right monogram, and date ΣΠΡ, *very good. Pl.* xxi, *No.* 1 s. 1·1

183 O same bust—℞ similar, date ΕΟΡ, *good* s. 1·1

184 O head of Demetrius, bearded, diademed—℞ Zeus seated on throne, holds Nike to left, *good. Pl.* xxi, *No.* 3 s. 1·2

185 O same head—℞ similar, *not good* s. 1·1

COPPER.

186 O head of Demetrius, beardless—℞ . . . . . ΤΟΡΟΣ, male figure grasping hand of city, *medium. Pl.* xxi, *No.* 8 s. ·75

187 O bust of Demetrius, beardless—℞ ΣΙΔΟ ΝΟΣ ΘΕΑΣ, and Phenician letters; city standing on prow with extended arm, date ΕΠΡ; *two coins, good. Pl.* xxi, *No.* 10 s. ·75

Copper Coins, *not in catalogue British Museum.*

188 O head of Demetrius, beardless . . . ΜΗΤΡΙΟΥ ΣΙΔΩΝΙΑC —℞ beak of galley, with Phenician inscription in three lines, one above and two under, *very good* s. ·7

*** Struck sideways, so that part of the Greek and Phenician letters are left out.

189 O head of Demetrius, radiate—℞ ΛΑΟΔΙΚΕΩΝ, and two lines of inscription, not legible, warrior standing and facing, holds spear, *not good* s. ·85

DEMETRIUS I or II.

LARGE COPPER COINS, WITH SERRATED EDGE.

190 ○ head of Apollo, with crown of laurel in border of dots
—℞ ΒΑΣΙΛΕΩΣ ΔΗΜΗΤΡΙΟΥ, tripod ; *three coins,*
very good *s.* 1

ALEXANDER II (ZEBINA).

SILVER.

191 ○ head of Alexander diademed, fillet border—℞ ΒΑΣΙ-
ΛΕΩΣ ΑΛΕΞΑΝΔΡΟΥ, Zeus seated on throne, holds
Nike and sceptre, to left monogram, below monogram,
in ex. date ΗΠΡ, *very good.* Type *Pl.* xxii, *No.* 2
s. 1·15

192 ○ same head—℞ similar, to left monogram, below AI,
very good *s.* 1·1

193 ○ same head—℞ similar, to left monogram, *plated, good*
s. 1·2

194 ○ same head—℞ similar, *plated?* to left ΙΣΙ, below Σ
and star, *medium* *s.* 1·2

195 ○ same head—℞ similar, to left monogram, below ΙΣ,
not good *s.* 1·1

196 ○ head of Alexander—℞ same inscriptions, two cornucopiæ united, *doubtful coin* *s.* ·7

COPPER.

197 ○ head of Alexander, diademed—℞ ΒΑΣΙΛΕΩΣ ΑΛΕΞ-
ΑΝΔΡΟΥ, young Dionysos standing, to left aplustre and
ΙΣΙ, date ΠΡ, *good.* *Pl.* xxii, *No.* 6 *s.* ·8

198 ○ head of Alexander, radiate—℞ same inscription, Pallas
armed to left, holds Nike, spear and shield, *good.* *Pl.*
xxii, *No.* 7 *s.* ·75

199 ○ same head—℞ same inscription, two cornucopiæ
united ; *three coins, one good, two medium.* *Pl.* xxii,
No. 9 *s.* ·8 *to* ·9

200 ○ head of Alexander in lion's skin—℞ same inscription,
Nike advancing to left, *medium.* *Pl.* xxii, *No.* 10
s. ·85

201 ☾ head of young Dionysius, wearing ivy wreath--℞
same inscription, Tyche, winged, holds rudder and
cornucopia, serrated edge, *very good. Pl.* XXII, *No.* 15
s. ·7

CLEOPATRA AND ANTIOCHUS VIII.

SILVER.

202 ☾ heads, jugated, of Cleopatra and Antiochus to right--
℞ ... ΑΝΤΙΟΧΟΥ ΒΑΣΙΛΙΣΣΗΣ ΚΛΕΟΠΑΤΡΑΣ,
eagle with closed wings on rudder, to left ΣΙΔ ΙΕΡ ΑΣΥ,
below monogram ; *heads good, reverse medium   s.* 1·15

203 ☾ same heads—℞ ΒΑΣΙΛΙΣΣΗΣ ΚΛΕΟΠΑΤΡΑΣ ΘΕΑΣ
ΚΑΙ ΒΑΣΙΛΕΩΣ ΑΝΤΙΟΧΟΥ, Zeus seated to left,
holds Nike and a sceptre, to left monogram, *good.*
Pl. XXIII, *No.* 3   *s.* 1·15

COPPER.

204 ☾ same heads—℞ same inscription, Nike advancing to
left, holding wreath, to left H, below aplustre ; *three
coins, one good, two medium. Pl.* XXIII, *No.* 4   *s.* ·7 *to* ·8

205 ☾ head of Antiochus, radiate—℞ same inscription, owl
on prostrate amphora ; *three coins, good. Pl.* XXIII,
No. 5   *s.* ·75

ANTIOCHUS VIII.

SILVER.

206 ☾ Bust of Antiochus to right—℞ ΑΝΤΙΟΧΟΥ ΒΑΣΙΛΕΩΣ,
eagle with closed wings to left on thunderbolt, over
shoulder palm, to left ΑΣ, dove and ΜΚ, date ϛqp,
good. Type of *Pl.* XXIII, *No.* 8, *Ascalon*   *s.* 1·1

207 ☾ head of Antiochus to right in border of dots—℞ same
inscription, eagle on thunderbolt to left, to left M, to
right date Γqp, *very good.* (*Not in Catalogue, B. M.*)
s. 1·1

208 ☾ same head—℞ similar, date Εqp, *good, but worn out
at edges.* (*Not in Catalogue, B. M.*)

209 ☾ head of Antiochus to right, in fillet border—℞ ΒΑΣΙ-
ΛΕΩΣ ΑΝΤΙΟΧΟΥ ΕΠΙΦΑΝΟΥΣ, Zeus draped, standing
to left, on head crescent, holds star and sceptre, to left
monogram, the whole in laurel wreath, *very good s.* 1·2

210 ☌ same head—℞ similar, to left monogram, *face very good, reverse slightly rubbed*   s. 1·1

211 ☌ same head—℞ similar, to left monogram, below date Eqp, *very good*   s. 1·15

212 ☌ same head—℞ similar, to left $\frac{I E}{A}$, *medium*   s. 1·15

213 ☌ same head—℞ similar, to left ΣΙΔ IEP and two monograms, in exergue, date Eqp, *good, but pierced* s. 1.15

214 ☌ same head—℞ similar, but Zeus naked, to left two monograms, *medium*   s. 1·15

COPPER.

215 ☌ head of Antiochus, radiate—℞ ΒΑΣΙΛΕΩΣ ΑΝΤΙΟΧΟΥ ΕΠΙΦΑΝΟΥΣ, eagle with closed wings to left, over shoulder sceptre, below aplustre and date Γqp, *very good*   s. ·75

216 ☌ same head—℞ similar, date not visible; *two coins, good*   s. ·75

ANTIOCHUS IX (Cyzicenus).

SILVER.

217 ☌ head of Antiochus to right, diademed—℞ ΒΑΣΙΛΕΩΣ ΑΝΤΙΟΧΟΥ ΦΙΛΟΠΑΤΟΡΟΣ, Pallas armed, standing to left, holds Nike, spear and shield, all within wreath, to left monogram, *very good*   s. 1·15

218 ☌ same head—℞ same inscription and type to left, monogram, date in ex. Σ, *very good*   s. 1·15

COPPER.

219 ☌ head of Antiochus, to right diad.—℞ same inscription, winged thunderbolt, date Σ; *two coins, very good.* Pl. xxv, *No.* 3   s. ·75

220 ☌ same head—℞ same inscription, Zeus seated to left, holds Nike and sceptre, *good.* Pl. xxv, *No.* 4   s. ·75

221 ☌ same head—℞ same inscription, figure standing to left, with extended arm holding spear with left, *good.* Pl. xxv, *No.* 5   s. ·85

222 ☌ bust of Eros, winged—℞ same inscription, Nike advancing to left, *two coins, good.* Pl. xxv, *No.* 9   s. ·7

223 O head of Pallas in helmet—℞ ΒΑΣΙΛΕΩΣ ΑΝΤΙΟΧΟΥ
ΦΙΛΟΠΑΤΟΡΟΣ. prow of vessel, *very good*. *Pl.* xxv,
No. 11   *s.* ·6

SELEUCUS VI (Epiphanes).

SILVER.

224 O head of Seleucus to right—℞ ΒΑΣΙΛΕΩΣ ΣΕΛΕΥΚΟΥ
ΕΠΙΦΑΝΟΥΣ (ΝΙΚΑΤΟΡΟΣ), (last line out of coin),
Zeus seated to left holds Nike and sceptre below Λ,
good. *Pl.* xxviii, *No.* 11   *s.* 1·05

COPPER.

225 O same head—℞ same inscription, Apollo standing
holds lyre ; rests elbow on column. *Pl.* xxv, *No.*
14   *s.* ·9

226 O same head—℞ same inscription, tripod Lebes, *medium*.
Pl. xxv, *No.* 15   *s.* ·9

ANTIOCHUS X (Eusebes).

SILVER.

227 O head of Antiochus to right diad. (no beard)—℞
ΒΑΣΙΛΕΩΣ ΑΝΤΙΟΧΟΥ ΕΥΣΕΒΟΥΣ ΦΙΛΟΠΑΤΟ-
ΡΟΣ, Zeus seated to left holds Nike and sceptre, in
wreath ; to left $\frac{\Sigma}{A}$, under seat monogram, *double struck*,
good. *Pl.* xxvi, *No.* 1   *s.* 1

COPPER.

228 O head of Antiochus with beard—℞ same inscription,
piles of Dioscuri, with straps,—above stars; *three coins*,
two very good. *Pl.* xxvi, *No.* 2   *s.* ·75

ANTIOCHUS XI (Philadelphus).

SILVER.

229 O head of Antiochus to right in fillet border—℞
ΒΑΣΙΛΕΩΣ ΑΝΤΙΟΧΟΥ ΕΠΙΦΑΝΟΥΣ, Zeus seated
to left, holds Nike and sceptre, all in wreath, to left $\overset{P}{E}$;
under Zeus monogram, *very good*. *Pl.* xxvi, *No.* 3
                                                               s. 1·2

230 ⊙ same head—℞ similar, *good* s. 1·05

231 ⊙ same head—℞ similar, under Zeus II, *very good*, s. 1·15

232 ⊙ same head—℞ ΒΑΣΙΛΕΩΣ ΑΝΤΙΟΧΟΥ ΕΠΙΦΑΝΟΥΣ ΦΙΛΑΔΕΛΦΟΣ, Zeus as above, to left monogram, below Δ, *not in the collection B. M.* s. 1·15

COPPER.

233 ⊙ same head, in border of dots—℞ ΒΑΣΙΛΕΩΣ ΑΝΤΙΟΧΟΥ ΕΠΙΦΑΝΟΥΣ, two cornucopiæ united, *good. Pl.* XXVI, *No.* 6 s. ·75

234 ⊙ same head—℞ same inscription, Tyche standing to left, holds rudder and cornucopia, *very good.* Type of *Pl.* XXV, *No.* 2, *not in the collection B. M.* s. ·6

235 ⊙ head of Antiochus to right, with beard—℞ ΒΑΣΙΛΕΩΣ ΑΝΤΙΟΧΟΥ ΕΠΙΦΑΝΟΥΣ ΦΙΛΑΔΕΛΦΟΣ, Pallas armed, holds in right Nike; in left spear and shield, *very good.* Type of *Pl.* XXVI, *No.* 8, *but larger and better* s. ·95

PHILIPPUS PHILADELPHUS.

SILVER.

236 ⊙ head of Philippus to right, diad. — ℞ ΒΑΣΙΛΕΩΣ ΦΙΛΙΠΠΟΥ ΕΠΙΦΑΝΟΥΣ ΦΙΛΑΔΕΛΦΟΥ, Zeus seated to left, holds Nike and sceptre, in wreath, to left monogram, below monogram, *very good* s. 1·1

237 Four other coins of the same type, with slight variations in size and shape, *all very good*

238 ⊙ same head—℞ similar, to left monogram, in ex. IE, *good* s. 1·1

239 ⊙ same head—℞ similar, to left monogram, *good* s. 1·1

239* ⊙ same head—℞ similar, to left monogram, below monogram, *barbarous*

DEMETRIUS III (Philopator).

SILVER.

240 ⊙ head of Demetrius to right, diad., bearded—℞ ΒΑΣΙΛΕΩΣ ΔΗΜΗΤΡΙΟΥ ΘΕΟΥ ΦΙΛΟΠΑΤΟΡΟΣ,

statue of Demeter, from shoulders rise ears of barley,
hands extended, in left three ears of barley, all in
wreath, to left monogram, in ex. date, ΘΙΣ   *s.* 1·05

241 Ꝍ same head—℞ similar, to left monogram in ex. date
AK (Σ)   *s.* 1·15

₊ These two very rare coins are covered with oxide of
silver, but *very good,* if cleaned.

COPPER.

242 Ꝍ head of Demetrius in diadem—℞ same inscription,
Hermes naked, holds caduceus and palm; *two coins,
not good. Pl.* XXVI, *No.* 12   *s.* ·7

243 Ꝍ head of Demetrius to right—℞ same inscription,
draped figure with helmet advancing to right, holds
palm over left shoulder, right arm extended, to left N.
in ex. date, ΞΙΣ in border of dots, *not in collection
B. M., very good*   *s.* ·8

ANTIOCHUS XII (DIONYSUS).

COPPER.

244 Ꝍ head of Antiochus to right, diadem—℞ ΒΑΣΙΛΕΩΣ
ΑΝΤΙΟΧΟΥ ΕΠΙΦΑΝΟΥΣ ΦΙΛΟΠΑΤΟΡΟΣ ΚΑΛΛΙ -
ΝΙΚΟΥ, Tyche to left, holds palm and cornucopia, *good.
Pl.* XXVII. *No.* 2   *s.* ·85

TIGRANES.

SILVER.

245 Ꝍ bust of Tigranes in Armenian tiara, on which star between two eagles in fillet border—℞ ΒΑΣΙΛΕΩΣ
ΤΙΓΡΑΝΟΥ, Antioch wearing mural crown, seated on
rocks holds in right palm, at her feet river Orontes
flowing, below monogram, *very good. Pl.* XXVII, *No.* 6
                                              s. 1·15

246 Ꝍ same head—℞ similar, to right, monogram below,
monogram, *good*   *s.* ·1

247 Ꝍ same head—℞ similar, slightly different in shape,
good

248 Ꝍ same head—℞ similar, *inscription barbarous, but very
fine*   *s.* 1·2

ALEXANDER THE GREAT.

SILVER TETRADRACHMS.

249　☽ head of Heracles (or Alexander in lion's skin) to right
—℞ ΑΛΕΞΑΝΔΡΟΥ, Jupiter on throne holding eagle ;
to left Phenician letters, *Act, fleur de coin*　　*s.* 1·1

250　☾ same head, very large, counter marked with anchor
of the Seleucid—℞ similar ; to left $\frac{A\Sigma}{K}$ *Ascalon, medium*　　*s.* 1·15

251　☾ same head, very large, counter marked with anchor—
℞ similar ; to left I Θ (?), *good*　　*s.* 1·25

252　☾ same head—℞ similar, under seat Σ, *good. Sidon, s.* 1·1

253　☽ same head—℞ similar, to left B ; under seat A Γ,
good. Berytus of Botrys　　*s.* 1·1

254　☾ same head—℞ similar, to left Victory holding wreath
under seat; monogram, *good. Laodicea*　　*s.* 1·10

255　☾ same head—℞ similar, to left monogram, *medium.
Aradus*　　*s.* 1·15

256　☽ same head—℞ similar, to left palm-tree ; under seat
AP, *medium. Tyre and Aradus*　　*s.* 1·15

257　☾ same head—℞ similar, to left forepart of a sheep,
good. Damascus　　*s.* 1·1

258　☽ same head—℞ ΒΑΣΙΛΕΩΣ ΑΛΕΞΑΝΔΡΟΥ, similar ;
to left Caducæ, under seat monogram, *good. Aradus
and Gabala ; Muller, No.* 1370　　*s.* 1·05

259　☾ same head—℞ ΑΛΕΞΑΝΔΡΟΥ, similar, to left flower
of Balaustium and ΗΦΑΙΣΣΙΩΝ, under seat P O,
Rhodes, very good　　*s.* 1·2

260　☽ same head—℞ similar, to left amphora, surrounded
by wreath and monograms, *medium. Temnos, Eolia*
　　s. 1·35

261　☽ same head—℞ similar, to left same amphora and
wreath, with monograms, *medium*　　*s.* 1·35

262　☾ same head—℞ similar, to left club in circle, under
Jupiter M P, *pierced, but good. Heraclea Sintica*

263　☽ same head—℞ ΒΑΣΙΛΕΩΣ ΑΛΕΞΑΝΔΡΟΥ, similar,
to left monogram in wreath ; under Jupiter Η, *very
good. Macedonia, Muller, No.* 711　　*s.* 1·15

264 ☉ same head—℞ similar, to left plough ; under seat monogram in wreath, *good. Macedonia, Muller, No.* 740

265 ☉ same head—℞ ΑΛΕΞΑΝΔΡΟΥ, similar, to left monogram; under seat Ε Υ, *good. Muller, No.* 1576 *s.* 1·1

266 ☉ same head—℞ ΒΑΣΙΛΕΩΣ ΑΛΕΞΑΝΔΡΟΥ, similar, to left monogram ; under seat R Y, *medium. Not in Muller s.* 1·05

267 ☉ same head—℞ ΒΑΣΙΛΕΩΣ ΑΛΕΞΑΝΔΡΟΥ, in legend around Jupiter, to left monogram, *good. Not in Muller s.* 1·5

268 ☉ same head—℞ ΑΛΕΞΑΝΔΡΟΥ, to left monogram ; under seat Σ I, *good. Not in Muller s.* ·1

COPPER.

269 ☉ same head—℞ ΑΛΕΞΑΝΔΡΟΥ, quiver, bow, and club ; under monogram ; *two coins, good, but barbarous in workmanship. Aradus s.* ·85

270 ☉ same head—℞ ΒΑΣΙΛΕΩΣ ΑΛΕΞΑΝΔΡΟΥ, similar, above club monogram, *very good s.* ·7

271 ☉ same head—℞ ΑΛΕΞΑΝΔΡΟΥ, similar ; *two coins, good s.* ·7

272 ☉ same head—℞ similar, *very good s.* ·55

PHILIPPUS ARIDÉE.

SILVER TETRADRACHMS.

273 ☉ head of Hercules (Alexander) — ℞ ΒΑΣΙΛΕΩΣ ΦΙΛΙΠΠΟΥ, to left monogram; under seat monogram, *very good. Phenicia, Muller, No.* 113 *s.* 1·05

274 ☉ same head—℞ similar, to left amphora ; under seat monogram, *good. Phenicia s.* 1·05

275 ☉ same head—℞ similar, to left club or stick ; under seat T, *good. Muller, No.* 81, *Northern Greece s.* 1·15

276 ☉ same head—℞ similar, to left M ; under seat monogram, *good. Mallus in Cilicia, Muller, No.* 154

COINS WITH PHENICIAN LETTERS.

277　☽ bearded head of Hercules or Melkart to right—℞.
galley on waves, with Phenician ciphers; *two coins,
good; thick silver*　　　　　　　　　　　　　　*s.* ·8

278　☽ lion devouring stag, circular Phenician legend—℞.
galley, under it marine horse; *silver*　　　　*s.* ·4

279　☽ bearded head of Melkart—℞. galley floating, Phenician
ciphers; *three coins, good; silver*　　　　　　*s.* ·3

280　☽ galley floating—℞. archer; *three coins, good; silver s.* ·3

281　☽ head of Bacchus (?)—℞. figure standing, holding indistinct object in right hand, to right and left Phenician
inscription, *good; copper*　　　　　　　　　*s.* ·85

282　☽ head of female with mural crown—℞. Victory seated
on rudder below; Phenician inscription (*copper*), *good*
　　　　　　　　　　　　　　　　　　　　　　s. ·7

283　☽ the same — ℞. aplustre and Phenician inscription
(*copper*), *good*　　　　　　　　　　　　　　*s.* ·5

KINGS OF EGYPT.

ALEXANDER AEGUS.

SILVER.

284　☽ head of Alexander diademed, horned and covered
with elephant's hide—℞. ΑΛΕΞΑΝΔΡΟΥ, Pallas advancing in fighting attitude; at her feet, eagle on
thunderbolt and monogram. Behind monogram, *very
good*　　　　　　　　　　　　　　　　　　　*s.* 1·1

285　☽ same head—℞. similar, before Pallas, eagle and monogram, *very good*　　　　　　　　　　　　　　*s.* 1·15

PTOLEMAEUS I.

286　☽ head of king radiate to left — ℞. ΠΤΟΛΕΜΑΙΟΥ
ΣΩΤΗΡΟΣ; eagle to left upon thunderbolt, to left
monogram (*silver*), *three coins, fleur de coin*
　　　　　　　　　　　　　　　　　s. 1·05 to 1·15

287　☽ same head—℞. same inscription and eagle; to left
monogram (*silver*), *barbarous but fleur de coin*　*s.* 1·1

288 O same head—℞ similar, with monograms ΚΛ and Φ Ι
(*silver*), *good*   *s*. 1·1
289 O same head—℞ ΠΤΟΛΕΜΑΙΟΥ ΒΑΣΙΛΕΩΣ, eagle to
left on thunderbolt ; to left monograms (Praetornium
and Rhinocurura) (*silver*), *good*   *s*. 1·1

PTOLEMAEUS II OR III (?).

290 O head of king to right diademed—℞ ΠΤΟΛΕΜΑΙΟΥ
ΒΑΣΙΛΕΩΣ, eagle to left on thunderbolt in border of
dots ; to left flower or helmet and date ΛΙ ; to right
ΚΙ (*silver*), *very good*   *s*. 1·05
291 O same head—℞ ΠΤΟΛΕΜΑΙΟΥ ΣΩΤΗΡΟΣ, eagle to
left ; to left monograms $\frac{TΠ}{ΣΩ}$ (Ptolemäis and Sozuza),
(*silver*), *not good*   *s*. 1·05

ARSINOÉ.

292 O head of queen to right, veiled and diademed behind
Κ—℞ ΑΡΣΙΝΟΗΣ ΦΙΛΑΔΕΛΦΟΥ, double cornucopia
(*silver*), *not good and out of shape*   *s*. 1·1

PTLOEMAEUS IV (PHILOPATOR.)

293 O bust of king as Dionysos—℞ ΠΤΟΛΕΜΑΙΟΥ. . . .
(struck sideways); eagle to left on thunderbolt (*silver*),
medium   *s*. ·7

PTOLEMAEUS V (EPIPHANOS.)

294 O bust of king diademed young, clad with chlamyde,
to right—℞ ΠΤΟΛΕΜΑΙΟΥ ΒΑΣΙΛΕΩΣ, eagle to
left ; to left Η (*silver*), *medium*   *s*. ·9

CLEOPATRA I.

295 O head of queen as Isis to right—℞ ΠΤΟΛΕΜΑΙΟΥ ;
eagle to left on thunderbolt (*copper*), *head very good,
reverse medium*   *s*. ·1

CLEOPATRA II.

296 O head of queen to right, covered with elephant's skin
—℞ ΠΤΟΛΕΜΑΙΟΥ ΒΑΣΙΛΕΩΣ ; eagle on thunder-
bolt to left (*copper*), *medium*   *s*. ·85

28

PTOLEMÄEUS VIII.

297 ☦ head of Jupiter Ammon to right—℞ ΒΑΣΙΛΕΩΣ
ΠΤΟΛΕΜΑΙΟΥ, two cornucopiae to left $\frac{\Sigma}{\Theta}$; to right
$\frac{\Omega}{E}$ (copper), medium   s. ·7

PTOLEMÄEUS IX.

298 ☦ head of king to right, covered with elephant's skin—
℞ ΠΤΟΛΕΜΑΙΟΥ ΒΑΣΙΛΕΩΣ, eagle to left (copper),
three coins, medium   s. ·9

PTOLEMÄEUS VIII or IX.

299 ☦ head of Jupiter Ammon to right—℞.... ΒΑΣΙΛΕΩΣ,
two eagles to left on thunderbolt (copper), not good
s. ·85

CLEOPATRA VII.

300 ☦ head of queen, diademed to right—℞ ΚΛΕΟΠΑΤΡΑΣ
ΒΑΣΙ.... eagle on thunderbolt to left; to left cornucopia; to right Π (copper), medium   s. 1·1

CLEOPATRA and MARCUS ANTONIUS.

301 ☦ bust of Cleopatra to left in border of dots, ΒΑΣΙΛΙССΑ
ΚΛΕΟΠΑΤ...—℞ head of Marcus Antonius to right
in border of dots (Greek legend, not very legible),
(silver), not good   s. 1·1

302 ☦ bust of queen to right, ... ΤΡΑΟ ΒΑΟΙΛΙ...—
℞... ΝΟС ΥΠΑΤΟΥ, head of Antoinus to right
(copper), struck sideways, but very good   s. ·8

UNCERTAIN COINS OF PTOLEMAI KINGS.

303 ☦ head of young king, diademed to right—℞ ΠΤΟΛΕ-
ΜΑΙΟΥ ΒΑΣΙΛΕΩΣ, eagle on thunderbolt to left,
ΙΛΙ; to right ΠΑ (silver and copper), medium   s. ·1

304 • head of Jupiter Ammon—℞ ΠΤΟΛΕΜΑΙΟΥ ΒΑΣΙ-
ΛΕΩΣ, eagle on thunderbolt to left; to left club;
between legs of eagle AP (*copper*), *good*   *s.* 1·4
305 • same head—℞ similar, to left cornucopia ; between
legs eagle, star (*copper*), *good*   *s.* 1·4
306 • same head—℞ similar, eagle with open wings to left ;
before eagle Σ and shield (*copper*), *good*   *s.* 1·1
307 • same head—℞ similar, eagle with closed wings ; before
eagle, flower ; between legs EYA (*copper*), *good*   *s.* ·9
308 • same head—℞ similar, before eagle, flower (*copper*),
good   *s.* ·65

ANTONINUS AND MARCUS AURELIUS (CÆSAR).

309 • ΑΥΤ. Κ. Τ. ΑΙΛ. ΑΔΡ ΑΝΤΟΝΙΝΟC CEB EYCE,
bust of Antoninus to right—℞ Μ ΑΥΡΗΛΙΟC ΚΑΙC
ΑΡ ΥΙΟC CEBAC., bust of Marcus Aurelius to right,
Alexandria (*copper*), *good*   *s.* 1·35

VARIOUS COINS OF EASTERN KINGS.

CASSANDER, KING OF MACEDONIA.

310 • head of Hercules to right — ℞ ΒΑΣΙΛΕΩΣ ΚΑΣ-
ΣΑΝΔΡΟΥ, horseman to right crowning horse's head
(*copper*), *good*   *s.* ·8
311 • head of Apollo—℞ same incription, horseman to
left ; to left, monogram ; to right, below horse, Μ
(*copper*), *good*   *s.* ·7
312 • young head, full face ; in middle, Macedonian shield
—℞ Β   (ΚΑ), helmet (*copper*), *good*   *s.* ·65
313 • same shield, without head—℞ Κ. helmet under, ear
of wheat (*copper*), *good*   *s.* ·55

ANTIGONUS GONATAS.

314 • Head of Pan ; in middle, Macedonian shield, orna-
mented with seven stars—℞ ΒΑΣΙΛΕΩΣ ΑΝΤΙΓΟΝΟΥ,
Pallas to left throwing thunderbolt ; to left, helmet ;
to right, ΤΙ (*silver*), *good*   *s.* 1·25

LYSIMACHUS.

315 ʘ horned head of Lysimachus to right—Ɽ ΒΑΣΙΛΕΩΣ ΛΥΣΙΜΑΧΟΥ, Pallas seated to left holding victory and leaning on shield (*silver*), *good*   *s.* 1·15

PRUSIAS.

316 ʘ head of Bacchus to right — Ɽ ΒΑΣΙΛΕΩΣ ΠΡΟΥ- ΣΕΙΟΥ, Centaur holding lyre to right ; to right, ΛΦ (*copper*), *very good*   *s.* ·85

NICOMEDUS III.

317 ʘ head of Nicomedus to right—Ɽ ΒΑΣΙΛΕΩΣ ΕΠΙΦΑ- ΝΟΥΣ ΝΙΚΟΜΙΙΔΟΥ, Jupiter to right holding crown in extended right hand, left leaning on hasta ; in front, eagle upon thunderbolt ; date, ΕΣ, and monogram (*silver*), *good*   *s.* 1·25

EUMENUS II.

318 ʘ head of king to right, with crown of laurel—Ɽ ΦΙΛΕ- ΤΑΡΟΥ Pallas seated to left leaning on shield, holds crown in extended right hand ; behind, bow ; to left, monogram (Ε ΥΜ) (*silver*), *medium*   *s.* 1·15

ATTALUS II.

319 ʘ head of king, diademed to right—Ɽ similar, right hand of Pallas rests on shield ; to left, bow (*silver*), *good*   *s.* 1·15

ARIARATHES VII.

320 ʘ head of king to right—Ɽ ΒΑΣΙΛΕΩΣ ΑΡΙΑΡΑΘΟΥ ΦΙΛΟΜΗΤΟΡΟΣ, Pallas to left holding Victory in right hand ; before, Ο. Μ.; behind, Λ ; *two coins* (*silver*), *good*   *s.* ·7

ARIOBARZANES I.

321 ʘ head of king to right—Ɽ ΒΑΣΙΛΕΩΣ ΑΡΙΟΒΑΡ.... (ΦΙΛΟ) ΡΟΜΑΙ (ΟΥ), same type ; before Pallas, mono- gram (*silver*), *good*   *s.* ·7

ARIOBARZANES II.

322 ℺ head of king to right — ℞ ΒΑΣΙΛΕΩΣ ΑΡΙΟΒΑΡ-
ΖΑΝ ... ΦΙΛΟΠΑΤΟ ... same type and size, *two coins*
(*silver*), *medium*   *s.* ·7

PARTHAN KING.

323 ℺ bust of king to left, with beard, on his head round
cap or helmet — ℞ ΒΑΣΙΛΕΩΣ ΜΕΓΑΛΟΥ ΔΙΧΑΙΟΥ
ΕΠΙΦΑΝΟΥΣ, forming a square, in centre of which
king seated to right holding bow (*silver*), *very good s.* ·75

MACEDONIA UNDER ROMAN RULE.

324 ℺ head, young and beardless, of Alexander the Great (?),
ΜΑΚΗΔΟΝΩΝ (the coin being struck sideways, only
part of the inscription is visible) — ℞ AESILLAS Q.,
club, seal, and recipient for silver, the whole in wreath
of laurel (*silver*), *fleur de coin*   *s.* 1·2

COIN OF ATHENS.

325 ℺ Head of Minerva to right — ΑΘΕ, owl, the whole in
hollow square (*silver*), *good but head of owl split   s.* ·1

ANTIOCHA AD ORONTEM.

AUTONOMOUS COINS IN COPPER.

326 ℺ head of Jupiter, laureated to right — ℞ ΑΝΤΙΟΧΕΩΝ
ΤΗΣ ΜΗΤΡΟΠΟΛΕΩΣ, Jupiter seated to left holding
victory; *three coins, very good*   *s.* ·95
327 ℺ same head — ℞ similar, *medium*   *s.* ·8
328 ℺ same head — ℞ same inscription, female figure standing to left holding cornucopia, right hand resting on
anchor, *medium*   *s.* ·65
   *** With dates of Actian era.
329 ℺ same head — ℞ ΑΝΤΙΟΧΕΩΝ ΕΠΙ ΟΥΑΡΟΥ, female
figure to right seated on rocks ; at her feet river swimming, date ΕΚ, *good*   *s.* ·8

330 O same head—℞ ΑΝΤΙΟΧΕΩΝ ΕΠΙ ΣΙΛΑΝΟΥ, date
ΔΜ, ram running to right, looking at star behind him,
good   *s.* '85
*** With dates of Cesarean era.

331 O veiled bust of city with mural crown, ΑΝΤΙΟΧΕΩΝ
—℞ ΕΠΙ ΚΟΥΑΔΡΑΤΟΥ. ET. ΔΡ., ram running to
right, looking at star and crescent behind him ; *three
coins, not good, but completing one another*   *s.* '8

332 O same head and legend—℞ altar with fire ET. ΔΙΡ., *very
good*   *s.* '75

333 O head of Jupiter, ΑΝΤΙΟΧΕΩΝ—℞ same altar ET ΖΙ,
good   *s.* '75

334 O same head and legend—℞ female seated to left,
throwing ball in a vase at her feet, ETO. EIP., *good s.* '75

335 O bust of female to right ΑΝΤΙΟΧΕΩΝ—℞ branch of
laurel, ETO. ΖΟΡ, *good*   *s* '6

336 O bust of female to right with mural crown—℞ S.C. in
wreath ; *two coins, medium*   *s.* '4

IMPERIAL COINS OF ANTIOCH.

AUGUSTUS.

337 O head of Augustus to right, ΚΑΙΣΑΡΙ ... ΑΡΧΙΕΡΕΙ
...—℞ ΑΡΧΙΕΡΑΤΙΚΟΝ ΑΝΤΙΟΧΕΙΣ ΖΚ, in four
lines in crown *(copper) good*   *s.* '95

338 O same head ΚΑΙΣΑΡΙ ΣΕΒΑΣΤΟ ΑΡΧΙΕΡ—℞ same
legend in three lines in ex. date Λ *(copper) good s.* 1·1

339 O head of Augustus to right ΚΑΙΣΑΡΟΣ ΣΕΒΑΣΤΟΥ
—℞ ΕΤΟΥΣ ΘΚ ΝΙΚΗΣ, Female to right seated on
rocks holding palm ; at her feet river swimming, two
monograms and ΙΓ *(silver) good*   *s.* '1

340 O the same—℞ ΕΤΟΥΣ ΖΚ ΝΙΚΗΣ, similar, two monograms and IB *(silver) medium*   *s.* '1

341 O head of Augustus to right, IMP AVGVST TR POT—
S.C. in crown of laurel *(copper) four coins, legends completing one another, medium*   *s.* '9 *to* 1

33

TIBERIUS.

342 ☊ head of Tiberius to right, legend indistinct · ℞ Λ ΕΠΙ
ΣΙΛΛΝΟΥ ΑΝΤΙΟΧΕΩΝ, in four lines, in crown of
laurel (*copper*), *not good*   *s.* 1·1

343 ☊ head of Tiberius to right, TI. CAESAR. AVG. TR.
POT. XXXIII—℞ S. C. in crown of laurel (*copper*)
medium   *s.* 1·05

CLAUDIUS.

344 ☊ head of Claudius to right, IMP. TI. CLAVD. AVG.
GER.—℞ S. C. in crown of laurel (*copper*), *good s.* 1·05

NERO.

345 ☊ bust of Nero to right, ΝΕΡΩΝΟΣ ΚΑΙΣΑΡΟΣ—☊
Eagle to left on thunderbolt ; to left palm, to right date
Η (P) (*silver*), *good*   *s.* 1·0✓

346 ☊ the same—℞ similar, to right date ΣΟΡ (*silver*), *two
coins, good*   *s.* 1·

347 ☊ same head to right, ΝΕΡΩΝ. ΚΑΙΣΑΡ. ΣΕΒΑΣΤΟΣ.
—℞ Eagle to right on thunderbolt ; to left palm,
ΕΤΟΥΣ. ΒΙΡ. Ι. (*silver*), *three coins, good*   *s.* 1·

348 ☊ head of Nero to right, IM. NER. CLAV. CAESAR
—℞ S. C. in crown of laurel (*copper*) *good*   *s.* 1·2

349 ☊ same head and legend—℞ similar (*copper*), *three coins,
good*   *s.* ·8✓

GERMANICUS AND . . . . .

350 ☊ head of Germanicus to right, GERMANICVS . . . .
AVG.—℞ head of Emperor (?), legend indistinct
(*silver*), *medium*   *s.* 1·

  ** With the exception of name of Germanicus, legend indistinct. The coin has the size, weight and shape of
the Antiochean coins ; but the Latin inscription on silver would be an anomaly.

GALBA.

351 ☊ head of Galba to right, ΑΥΤΟΚΡΑΤΩΡ ΣΕΡΟΥΙΟΣ
ΓΑΛΒΑΣ ΣΕΒΑΣΤΟΣ—℞ eagle holding crown in
beak resting on branch of laurel ; to left palm in ex.
ΕΤΟΥΣ. Β. (*silver*) *good*   *s.* 1·1

D

352 ○ same head, ΑΥΤΟΚΡΑΤΩΡ ΓΑΛΒΑϹ ΚΑΙϹΑΡ
ϹΕΒΑϹΤΟϹ—℞ similar, ΕΤΟΥϹ. B. (silver), good s. 1·1
353 ○ same head, ΓΑΛΒΑϹ .... ΒΑϹΤΟϹ—℞ eagle
to left on thunderbolt; to left palm, ΕΤΟΥϹ ... (silver),
medium s. 1·05

OTHO.

354 ○ head of Otho to right, ΑΥΤΟΚΡΑΤΟΡ ΜΑΡΚΟϹ.
ΟΘΩΝ. ΚΑΙϹΑΡ. ϹΕΒΑϹΤΟϹ.—℞ eagle to left hold
ing crown in beak, resting on branch of laurel; to left
palm in ex. ΕΤΟΥϹ. A. (silver) good s. 1·1
355 ○ same head, ΑΥΤΟΚΡΑΤΩΡ. Μ. ΟΘΩΝ. ΚΑΙϹΑΡ.
ϹΕΒΑϹΤΟϹ.—℞ similar, same date (silver) good s. 1·
356 ○ same head and legend—℞ similar, but no date (silver)
medium s. 1·
357 ○ head of Otho to right, M.M. OTHO ... AE. AVG.
℞ S.C. in crown of laurel (copper) not good s. 1·2

VESPASIAN.

358 ○ head of Vespasian to right, ΑΥΤΟΚΡΑ. ΟΥΕϹΠΑ-
ϹΙΑΝΟϹ. ΚΑΙϹΑΡ ϹΕΒΑϹΤΟϹ.—℞ eagle to left,
holds crown in beak, rests on branch of laurel; to left
palm, in ex. ΕΤΟΥϹ. A. (silver) good s. 1·1
359 ○ same head, ΑΥΤΟΚΡΑ. ΟΥΕϹΠΑϹΙΑΝΟϹ. ΚΑΙϹΑΡ.
ϹΕΒΑϹΤΟϹ—℞ eagle to left on club; before it palm,
ΕΤΟΥϹ. ΝΕΟΥ. ΙΕΡΟΥ. Β. (silver) medium s.1·05
360 ○ same head, but part of legend out of coin—℞ similar
(silver) medium s. ·95
361 ○ same head and legend—℞ eagle to left on thunderbolt, before palm, ΕΤΟΥϹ. ΝΕΟΥ. ΙΕΡΟΥ. Β. (silver)
medium s. 1·
362 ○ same head ΑΥΤΟΚΡΑΤ ΚΑΙϹΑ ΟΥΕϹΠΑϹΙΑΝΟΥ—
℞ similar, ΕΤΟΥϹ. A. (silver) medium s. 1·
363 ○ same head and legend—℞ same eagle to right, ΙΕΡΟΥ
...... (silver) medium s. ·95
364 ○ bust of Vespasian to left, ΟΥΕϹΠΑϹΙΑΝΟϹ. ΚΑΙϹΑΡ.
ϹΕΒΑϹΤΟϹ.—℞ eagle with spread wings upon altar,
ΕΤΟΥϹ. ΝΕΟΥ. ΙΕΡΟϹ. (Δ ?) (silver) medium s. 1·

365 O head of Vespasian to left, IMP. CAESAR. VES-
PASIAN AVG.—℞ S. C. in crown of laurel, (*copper*) ;
two coins, good   *s.* 1·15

366 O the same—℞ similar (*copper*) ; *two coins, medium s.* ·85

367 O bust of Vespasian to right IMP. CAES. VESP.
AVG. P. M. COS. IIII—℞ S. C. in crown of laurel
(*copper*), *good*   *s.* 1·

TITUS.

368 O head of Titus to right, CAESAR. IMP. PONT.—℞
S. C. in crown of laurel (*copper*) ; *two coins, medium*
                                                                    s. 1·1

VESPASIAN AND TITUS.

369 O ΑΥΤΟΚΡΑΤ. ΚΑΙΣΑ. ΟΥΕΣΠΑΣΙΑΝΟΥ, head of
Vespasianus to left, below eagle with spread wings—℞
ΦΛΑΥΙ. ΟΥΕΣΠ. ΚΑΙΣ. ΕΤΟΥΣ. ΝΕΟΥ. ΙΕΡΟΥ., head
of Titus to right ; to right B. (*silver*) ; *two coins, one
good and one medium*   *s.* 1·

DOMITIANUS.

370 O ΑΥΤΟΚ. ΚΑΙΣΑΡ. ΔΟΜΙΤΙΑΝΟΣ. ΣΕΒ. ΓΕΡΜ., head
of Domitianus to right—℞ ΕΤΟΥC. ΝΕΟΥ. ΙΕΡΟΥ. Η̄
eagle upon thunderbolt to right ; before it palm,
(*silver*), *good*   *s.* 1·05

371 O the same—℞ similar, date Z̄. (*silver*), *medium*   *s.* 1·

372 O (IMP. DOMITIA) NVS. CAESAR. AVG., head of
Domitian to right—℞ S. C. in crown of laurel (*copper*),
good   *s.* 1·

373 O DOMITIANVS . . . . head of Domitian to
left—℞ S. C. in crown of laurel (*copper*), *good*   *s.* ·9

NERVA.

374 O IMP. CAESAR. NER (VA), head of Nerva to right
—℞ S. C. in crown of laurel, below A. (*copper*),
medium   *s.* 1·1

TRAJAN.

375 O ΑΥΤ. ΚΑΙC. ΝΕΡ. ΤΡΑΙΑΝΟC. CΕΒ. ΓΕΡΜ. ΔΑΚ,
head of Trajan to right—℞ ΔΗΜΑΡΧ. ΕΞ. ΥΠΑΤ.,
date Σ, eagle with spread wings, head to right, holding
crown in beak (*silver*) ; *two coins, good*   *s.* 1·

D 2

376 ○ the same—℞ similar, date E, (*silver*), *good*   *s.* 1

377 ○ same inscription, head of Trajan to right, below eagle and club—℞ same inscription, bust of Hercules, with lion's skin around neck (*silver*) ; *four coins of different dies, good*   *s. '9 to 1'*

378 ○ the same—℞ same inscription, date E (*silver*) ; *two coins, good*   *s.* 1'

379 ○ the same, club before face—℞ similar, date not visible, (*silver*) ; *two coins, good*   *s.* 1'

380 ○ the same, eagle and club before head—℞ same inscription, city of Antioch seated on rocks to right, at her feet river swimming, date E. (*silver*) ; *two coins, good*   *s.* 1'

381 ○ AYTOKP. KAIC. NEP. TPAIANOC. CEB. ΓEPM. ΔAK, head of Trajan to right—℞ S. C. in crown of laurel, date I. (*copper*), *good*

382 ○ the same—℞ similar, date Θ (*copper*) ; *medium*

383 ○ .... OKP. KAIC. TPAIANOC., head of Trajan to right—℞ S. C. in crown, date A. (*copper*), *medium s.* ·8

384 ○ .... KAIC. TPAIANOC., same head—℞ similar; date B. (*copper*), *medium*   *s.* ·8

HADRIAN.

385 ○ AYT. KAI. ΘE. TPA. ΠAP. YI. ΘE. YI. TPAI. ΛΔPIANOC. CEB., bust of Hadrian in armour to right—℞ ΔHMAPX. EΞ. YΠAT. B., eagle upon leg of quadruped (*silver*) ; *two coins, good*   *s.* 1'

386 ○ the same—℞ similar, with palm to right ; date not visible (*silver*), *good*   *s.* 1'

387 ○ same inscription and head—℞ S. C. in crown ; below E. S. (*copper*), *good*   *s.* 1'1

ANTONINUS THE PIOUS.

388 ○ ... KAI TI AIA. AΔP. (ANTΩNEINOC, out of coin), head of Antoninus to right—℞ S. C. in crown, below A. (*copper*), *medium*   *s.* '9

389 ○ the same—℞ similar, date Δ. (*copper*), *medium s.* '95

390 ○ the same—℞ similar, date Ϛ. (*copper*), *not good s.* '9

37

MARCUS AURELIUS.

391 Ꙩ AYT. KAI. ANTΩNEINOC, head of Marcus Aurelius to right—℞ S. C., below eagle and B; the whole in wreath, *medium*   *s.* '9

COMMODUS.

392 Ꙩ AYT. KAIC. KOMMOΔOC. CEB., head of Commodus to right—Ꙩ CPCAP ΔHMAPX. EΞ. YΠATOC B, eagle with head to left on thunderbolt, to left head of sheep, to right star (*silver*), *good*   *s.* 1·05

SEPTIMUS SEVERUS.

393 Ꙩ AYT. KAI. CEOYHPOC, CEB., bust of Septimus Severus to right—℞ ΔHMAPX. EΞ. YΠATOC. Γ., eagle with head to left, holding animal in beak; between leg, star, (*silver*), *very good*   *s.* 1·

CARACALLA.

394 Ꙩ AYT. K. M. A. ANTΩNEINOC. CEB., head of Caracalla to right—℞ ΔHMAPX. EΞ. YΠATOC. TO. Δ., eagle with head to right, holding crown in beak, and in claws head of bull (*silver*), *good*   *s.* 1·

395 Ꙩ the same—℞ similar, date not visible; eagle looking to left; between legs, star   *s.* 1·05

GETA.

396 Ꙩ AYT. KAI. ΓETAC. CEB, head of Geta to right— ℞ ΔHMAPX. EΞ YΠATOC. TO. B. eagle looking to left holding crown in beak; on each side of head, stars (*silver*), *very good*   *s.* 1·05

397 Ꙩ similar—℞ similar (hole on the top of head) (*silver*), *good*   *s.* 1·05

MACRIN.

398 Ꙩ AYT. K. MA. OΠ CE. MAKPINOC, head of Macrin to right—℞ ΔHMAPX. EΞ YΠATOC. Δ, eagle looking to left holding crown in beak; below BE (*adulterated silver*), *medium*   *s.* 1·

399 Ꙩ the same—℞ similar, star between legs of eagle (*adulterated silver*), *medium*   *s.* 1·05

DIADUMENIANUS.

400 O ΛΥΤ . Κ . Μ . ΟΠ . Δ . ΑΝΤΩΝΕΙΝΟC, bust of Diadumenianus to right, draped with radiate crown on head
—℞ ΔΗΜΑΡΧ . ΕΞ . ΥΠΑΤΟC, eagle looking to
right; between legs, lion walking to right (*adulterated
silver*), *very good* s. 1·1

401 O ΑΥΤ . ΚΑΙ . Μ . ΔΙΑ . ΑΝΤΩΝΕΙΝΟC . bust of Diadumenianus to right—℞ S. C. in crown; above Δ
(*copper*), *good* s. ·8

ELAGABALUS.

402 O ΛΥΤ . Κ . ΜΛ . ΑΝΤΩΝΕΙΝΟC . CEB . bust of Elagabalus, draped to left—℞ ΔΗΜΑΡΧ . ΕΞ . ΥΠΑΤΟC .
ΤΟ . Β . eagle looking to left, holding crown in beak;
between legs, star; on sides of head, A . E . (*adulterated silver*), *very good* s. 1·15

403 O similar head, to right—℞ similar (*adulterated silver*),
medium s. ·95

ALEXANDER SEVERUS.

404 O ΑΥΤ . ΚΑΙ . Μ . ΑΡ . ΑV . CE . ΑΛΕΞΑΝΔΡΟC, bust
of Alexander, to right—℞ ΑΝΤΙΟΧΕΩΝ ΜΗΤ .
female, seated on rocks, to left, at her feet, river,
swimming; above, ram, running to left, Δ . E . S . C .
(*copper*), *very good* s. 1·35

405 O the same—℞ similar, star before figure (*copper*), *medium*
s. 1·25

406 O the same—℞ same inscription, female seated on rocks
crowned by figures standing behind; in front, figure
of Fortune with cornucopia; below, river swimming and
Π . (*copper*), *medium* s. 1·25

GORDIANUS III.

407 O ΑΥΤΟΚ . Κ . Μ . ΑΝΤ . ΓΟΡΔΙΑΝΟC . CEB . bust of
Gordianus, to right—℞ ΔΗΜΑΡΧ . ΕΞ . ΟΥCΙΑC,
eagle looking to left, holding crown in beak; below,
S . C . (*adulterated silver*), *very good, but pierced* s. 1·05

PHILIPPUS, THE FATHER.

408 Ↄ AYTOC . K . M . IOYA . ΦIΛIΠΠOY . C . EB . head
of Philippus, to right—℞ ΔHMAPX . EΞ . OYCIAC .
eagle looking to left, S . C . below, MONETA (*adulterated silver*), *medium* s. 1·05

409 Ↄ same legend, head of Philippus with radiate crown, to
right—℞ ANTIOXEΩN MHTPO . KOΛΩ, female
head with mural crown to right ; above, ram running,
ΔE . and S . E . (*copper*), *very good* s. 1·25

410 Ↄ the same, head of Emperor not radiate—℞ similar
(*copper*), *very good* s. 1·15

411 Ↄ the same, head of Emperor to left—℞ similar (*copper*),
good s. 1·15

PHILIPPUS, THE SON.

412 Ↄ AYTOK . K . M . IOYAI . ΦIΛIΠΠOC . CEB., head of
Philippus to right—℞ ΔHMAPX . EΞ OYCIAC . YΠA
TOC . Δ, eagle to left, below ANTIOXIA, (*adulterated
silver*), *good* s. 1·05

413 Ↄ the same—℞ ANTIOXEΩN . MHTPO . KOΛON., female with mural crown to right, above ram to right,
ΔE and S.C. (*copper*), *good* s. 1·15

414 Ↄ the same, head of Emperor radiate—℞ similar (*copper*),
good s. 1·10

TRAJANUS DECIUS.

415 Ↄ AYT . K . Γ . ME . KY. ΔEKIOC . TPAIANOC . CEB.,
radiate head of Decius to right—℞ ΔIIMAPX . EΞ .
OYCIAC., eagle to left, below S.C. (*adulterated silver*),
very good s. 1·1

HERENNIUS ETRUSCUS, CAESAR.

416 Ↄ EPENN . ETPOY . MEKY . ΔEKIOC . KECAP., bust
of Etruscus to right, head unadorned—℞ ANTIOXEΩN.
MHTPO . KOΛΩN., temple with female seated in the
middle, above ram running, below S.C. (*copper*), *good*
s. 1·25

HOSTILIANUS, CAESAR.

417 Ѻ Γ. ΟΥΛ. OCTIΛIΛN. ME. ΚΥΙΝΤΟϹ. ΚΕϹΑΡ., head
of Hostilianus to right, unadorned—℞ ΔΗΜΑΡΧ.
EΞ. OYCIAC., eagle to left, S.C. *(adulterated silver),
very good*   *s.* 1·05

TREBONIANUS GALLUS.

418 Ѻ ΑΥΤ. Κ. Γ. OYIB. ΤΡΕΒ. ΓΑΛΛΟϹ. ϹΕΒ. bust of
Trebonianus to right—℞ ΔΗΜΑΡΧ. ΕΞΟΥϹΙΑϹ.
ΥΠΑΤΟ. Β. eagle looking to right ; between legs Γ ;
below S. C. *(adulterated silver), medium*   *s.* 1·05
419 Ѻ the same—℞ ΔΗΜΑΡΧ. ΕΞ. OYCIAC. eagle to left
(adulterated silver), good   *s.* 1·05
420 Ѻ the same—℞ ΑΝΤΙΟΧΕΩΝ. ΜΗΤΡΟ. ΚΟΛΩΝ.
temple, with female seated in centre ; above, ram running, and Δ. E. below, river swimming, and S. C.
(copper), very good   *s.* 1·15

TREBONIANUS GALLUS AND VOLUSIANUS.

421 Ѻ ΑΥΤΟΚ. OYIB. ΤΡΕΒ. ΓΑΛΛΟϹ ΚΑΙ. ΟΥΟΛΟΥ-
ϹΙΑΝΟϹ. ϹΕΒ. busts of Trebonianus and Volusianus,
face to face—℞ ΑΝΤΙΟΧΕΩΝ. ΜΗΤΡ. ΚΟΛΩΝ.
temple, with female seated in middle ; above, ram ;
below, river swimming, and S. C. *(copper), very good,
but pierced*   *s.* 1·2

BERYTUS.

AUTONOMOUS COINS, IN COPPER.

422 Ѻ head of female, with mural crown to right—℞ ΒΗ.
Neptune holding trident upon sea horses to left ; *three
coins, two good, one inferior*   *s.* ·8
423 Ѻ same head (countermark on head)—℞ ΒΗΡΥ. dolphin
holding trident ; on both sides caps of Dioscuri ; *two
coins, medium*   *s.* ·8

424 ☾ dolphin holding trident—℞ vase and monograms, *medium*   *s.* ·6

425 ☾ COL . Silenus carrying wine skin—℞ BER, prow of galley ; *two coins, good*   *s.* ·55

COLONIAL COINS IN COPPER.

AUGUSTUS.

426 ☾ AVGVSTVS .. head of Augustus to right—℞ COL . IVL, colonist leading two oxen to right, *good*   *s.* 1·15

427 ☾ IMP . CAESAR . AVGVSTVS . head of Augustus to right—℞ COL . IVL . colonist leading two oxen to left ; *two coins, one good, one inferior*   *s.* ·9

428 ☾ IMP . AVG . head of Augustus to right—℞ similar ; *two coins, medium*   *s.* ·7

429 ☾ DIVOS . AVGVSTVS, head of Augustus to right—℞ two legionary eagles and ensigns; above, $\frac{COL}{V}$; below, $\frac{BER}{VIII}$ *very good*   *s.* ·75

TIBERIUS.

430 ☾ legend indistinct, head of Tiberius to right—℞ COL . IVL . AVG . colonist leading two oxen to right, *medium*   *s.* 1·05

CLAUDIUS.

431 ☾ IMP . TI . CLAVD . CAESAR . AVG . GERM . head of Claudius to right—℞ COL . IVL . colonist leading two oxen to right ; *two coins, black patine, very fine s.* ·95

432 ☾ same head to left, legend indistinct—℞ similar, *not good*   *s.* ·9

433 ☾ TI . CLAVDIVS . CAESAR . same head to left—℞ two military ensigns and eagles . V . VIII ; *two coins, good s.* ·8

NERVA.

434 ☾ DIVVS NERVA, head of Nerva to right—℞ COL . BER . Neptune standing to left, right foot on rock, holding dolphin and trident, *medium*   *s.* 1·

435 ☾ ... NERVA ... head of Nerva to right—℞ COL . IVL . AVG . FEL . BER . on four sides of colonist leading two oxen ; *four coins, one good, three inferior s.* ·9

TRAJAN.

436   ℞ ... NER. TRAIAN, head of Trajan to right ℞
COL. IVL. AVG. FEL. BER, on four sides of colonist, leading two oxen, *medium*   *s.* 1·15

437   ℞ ... TRAIN. AVG. GERM. DAC. COS. VI. head
of Trajan to right—℞ COL. BER. colonist leading
two oxen to right, *black patine, very fine*   *s.* 1·

₊ Two similar coins, legend on side of head only partly
legible ; reverses good.

438   ℞. NER. TRAIANOC. AVG. GERM. head of Trajan
to right—℞ COL. IVL. AVG. BER. Neptune to left,
holding dolphin and trident, *good*   *s.* 1·

439   ℞ same legend and head—℞ COL. BER. same type of
Neptune holding dolphin and trident; *two coins, medium*
    s. 1·

440   ℞ same head, only part of legend legible—℞ COL.
BER. two military ensigns and eagles in crown of
leaves ; *three coins, medium*   *s.* ·9

441   ℞ head of Trajan to right, legend erased—℞ COL. IVL.
AVG. FEL. BER. Astarte in temple crowned by
victory on stand, *medium*   *s.* 1·2

HADRIANUS.

442   ℞ IMP. CAES. TRAI. HADRIANVS. AVG. P.P.,
head of Hadrian to right—℞ COL (sic) two military
ensigns and eagles in crown of leaves, *very fine*   *s.* ·9

443   ℞ the same—℞ COL. BER., similar, *medium*   *s.* ·9

444   ℞ the same—℞ COL. BER., similar, *very fine*   *s.* ·75

MARCUS AURELIUS AND LUCIUS VERUS.

445   ℞ IMP. .. M. AVR. ANTONINVS. AVG., head of
Marcus Aurelius to left below, eagle, in centre COL.—
℞ IMP. CAESAR.., head of Verus to right, below,
eagle, and BER, *medium*   *s.* 1·05

446   ℞ IMP. CAESAR. M. AVR. ANTONINVS. AVG ; in
ex. COL, head of Marcus Aurelius to right—℞ IMP.
CAES. AVG. VERVS. AVG., head of Verus to right,
in ex. BER., *good*   *s.* ·95

COMMODUS.

447 ○ IMP... COMMODVS. ANTONINVS., head of
Commodus to right—℞ Astarte in middle of temple
crowned by Victory, standing on column, to left, SEC.
to right, SAEC. in ex. COL. BER, *medium*   s. 1·

448 ○ legend erased, head of Commodus to right—℞ Neptune to left holding dolphin and trident, SEC. SAEC.
in middle COL. BER ; *four coins, not good*   s. ·95

449 ○ same head—℞ COL. BER., two ensigns and eagles
in crown, *not good*   s. ·85

SEPTIMUS SEVERUS and CARACALLA.

450 ○ legend erased, busts of Septimus Severus, and Caracalla face to face—℞ Astarte in temple crowned by
Victory standing on column, in ex. COL. BER. ; *two
coins, not good*   s. 1·

CARACALLA.

451 ○ legend partly erased, head of Caracalla to right—℞
Astarte in temple crowned by Victory, in ex. COL.
BER. ; *three coins, medium*   s. ·8 *to* 1·

452 ○ same head to right—℞ COL. BER., Neptune to left
holding dolphin and trident, *not good*   s. ·8

ELAGABALUS.

453 ○ IMP. CAESAR. M. AVR. ANTONINVS. AVG.,
head of Elagabalus to left—℞ temple with four columns and triangular roof ; in middle Astarte crowned
by Victory on stand ; to right and left two smaller
figures ; on top of temple, Neptune, and female kneeling ; below two small figures upon dolphins, around :
COL. IVL. AVG. FEL. BER., *very fine*   s. 1·2

454 ○ same head and legend—℞ similar, *good*   s. 1·2

455 ○ same head and legend—℞ temple with four columns
and curved roof, in middle winged figure, above, man
on horseback, around, COL. IVL. AVG. FEL., in ex.
BER. ; *three coins, good*   s. 1·2

456 ☉ same head and legend—♃ similar ; *two coins good s.* 1·

457 ☉ same head and legend—♃ Neptune and female
kneeling ; around, COL. IVL. AVG. FEL., in ex.
BER., *medium*   *s.* 1·2

458 ☉ same head, legend partly erased—♃ Hercules as a
child, struggling with two serpents, COL. IVL. AVG.
BER. ; *two coins, medium*   *s.* 1·

459 ☉ same head, legend partly erased—♃ BER., in middle
of circle formed by eight cabires ; below, galley, *not
very good*   *s.* 1·

460 ☉ same head and legend—♃ temple, in middle of which
Neptune, holding dolphin and trident ; *two coins, one
good, one inferior*   *s.* ·9

GORDIANUS III.

461 ☉ IMP. CAES. M. ANT. GORDIANVS. AVG. COS.
II, bust of Gordianus to right—♃ bust of Astarte in
middle of temple ; on the top, Hercules and female
kneeling, on both sides small figures with extended
arms ; in ex. quadruped, COL. IVL. AVG. FEL.
BER. ; *five coins, good and medium*   *s.* 1·1

462 ☉ same head and legend—♃ same inscription, Bacchus
standing, holding spear and cornucopia ; *three coins,
good and medium*   *s.* ·8

463 ☉ same head and legend—♃ COL. BER., Neptune
holding dolphin and trident, *good*   *s.* ·7

GALLIENUS.

464 ☉ IMP. C. P. LIC. GALLIENVS. VER., head of Gallienus to right—♃ COL. IVL. AVG. FEL. BER.,
Astarte standing, holding spear in right and crowned
by Victory ; *three coins, medium*   *s.* 1·15

465 ☉ same legend (only partly visible) and head—♃ same
inscription, lion going to left ; *two coins, not good s.* 1·

TYRUS.

AUTONOMOUS SILVER COINS.

466 O head of Hercules, with crown of laurels to right, in circle of dots—℞ ΤΥΡΟΥ ΙΕΡΑC ΚΑΙ ΑΣΙΛΟΥ, eagle to left, upon rudder, palm over shoulder, to right monogram, to left club and L. B. (year 2), *very good*   *s.* 1·1

467 O the same—℞ similar, between legs of eagle monogram, date L. Γ. (year 3), *very good*   *s.* 1·1

468 O the same—℞ similar, between legs of eagle M, date L. Δ (year 4), *very good*   *s.* 1·2

469 O the same—℞ similar, date L. ς. (year 6), *very good*   *s.* 1·1

470 O the same—℞ similar, to right monogram, date L. Z. (year 7), *good*   *s.* 1·15

471 O the same—℞ similar (Didrachmes), date L. Z. (year 7), *very good*   *s.* ·85

472 O the same—℞ similar, to right M, date L. H. (year 8), *very good*   *s.* 1·15

473 O the same—℞ similar, date L. Θ. (year 9), *very good*   *s.* 1·15

474 O the same—℞ similar, to right Z. B., date L. I. (year 10), *very good*   *s.* 1·1

475 O the same—℞ similar, to right monogram, date A I (year 11), *very good*   *s.* 1·25

476 O the same—℞ similar, to right Z B, date Γ I (year 13), *very good*   *s.* 1·15

477 O the same—℞ similar (Didrachme), date Δ I (year 14), *good*   *s.* ·8

478 O the same—℞ similar, to right monogram, date ς I (year 16), *very good*   *s.* 1·15

∗ These Tetradrachms, of remarkable workmanship, and which are in a beautiful state of preservation, are probably among the first which have been struck after the privilege of autonomy had been conceded to Tyre by Demetrius II.

AUTONOMOUS COINS IN COPPER.

479 ℺ head of Hercules to right, with crown of laurels—℞ club, at the end of which, monogram of Tyre, ΜΗΤΡΟ ΠΟΛΕΩΣ to right and left of club, below Phenician letters, *good*   *s.* ·9

480 ℺ the same—℞ same club, with ΜΗΤΡΟ ΠΟΛΕΩΣ written around, the whole in wreath of leaves; *two coins, medium*   *s.* ·9

481 ℺ head of female, with mural crown to right, to right B —℞ galley and $\frac{ΑΤΣΡΥ}{ΙΕΡΑC}$ below Phenician letters, *very good*   *s.* ·8

482 ℺ head of female, with mural crown to right—℞ ΜΗΤΡΟ- ΠΟΛΕΩΣ ΙΕΡΑC, palm tree, ΑΣ; *four coins, good*   *s.* ·65

483 ℺ the same—℞ rudder of galley and Phenician inscription in three lines, *good*   *s.* ·7

484 ℺ the same—℞ Astartea to left, standing upon galley, behind monogram of Tyre; *two coins, good*   *s.* ·5

COLONIAL COINS.

485 ℺ bust of Septimus Severus to right, SEPT. SEVERVS. AVG. IMP.—℞ SEP. TYRVS. METROP..... colonist leading two oxen to right, LEG. III. GAL. upon vexillum, *good*   *s.* 1·35

486 ℺ bust of Elagabalus to right, IMP. CAES. M. AV. ANTONINVS. AVG.—℞ TYRIORVM., Astartea standing, right hand upon trophy, to right Victory upon stand presents crown to her, below palm tree and murex, *very good*   *s.* 1·15

487 ℺ the same—℞ SEP. TYRVS. METROP ... similar type, below, to right, Silenus; *two coins, medium*   *s.* 1· and 1·2

488 ℺ head of Gallienus to right, IMP. C. P. LIC. GAL- LIENVS. AVG.—℞ COL. TYRO. MET., Astartea as above, *good*   *s.* 1·7

489 ℺ the same—℞ same legend, bust of Goddess in temple with circular roof, before head star, *good*   *s.* 1·15

490 ℺ the same—℞ same legend, female to left seated on shield, holds Victory in right hand, left rests upon spear, *not good*   *s.* 1·1

491 ℺ head of Valerianus to right, IMP. C. P. LIC. VALE-RIANVS. AVG.—℞ COL. TYRO. METR., snake encircling an egg, *good*   *s.* 1·05

492 ℺ the same—℞ same legend, figure holding cornucopia, *not good*   *s.* 1·15

493 ℺ the same—℞ same legend, table with urns for games, below ERACLIA, *not good*   *s.* 1·2

SIDON.

AUTONOMOUS COINS.

494 ℺ head of female to right, with mural crown and veil— ℞ ΣΙ (ΔΩΝΙΩΝ) ΙΕΡΑΣ ΚΑΙ ΑΣΙΛΟΥ, eagle to left, date L. ΘΝ. to right, monogram, *silver, not good*   *s.* 1·15

COPPER COINS.

495 ℺ head of female to right, with mural crown and veil— ℞ ΣΙΔΩΝΙΩΝ, Astartea to left, upon galley, L. ΛΑ; *two coins, medium*   *s.* ·8

496 ℺ same head — ℞ ΣΙΔΩΝΙΩΝ ΘΕΑΣ, galley (under) ΙΕΡΑΣ ΚΑΙ ΑΣΙΛΟΥ ΚΑΙ ΝΑΥΑΡΧΙΑΟΣ, *good*   *s.* ·9

497 ℺ same head—℞ ΣΙΔΩΝΙΩΝ. L. Γ., galley; below, Phenician letters, *medium*   *s.* ·9

498 ℺ same head—℞ ΣΙΔΩΝΩΣ ΘΕΑΣ, galley; *six coins, with different dates, medium*   *s.* ·6

499 ℺ head of Bacchus to right—ΣΙΔΩΝΩΣ ΘΕΑΣ, vase in crown of leaves, date ΖΚΣ ; *two coins, good*   *s.* ·7

500 ℺ same head to left—℞ similar, *good*   *s.* ·7

501 ℺ head of Jupiter to left—℞ ΣΙΔΩΝΙΩΝ, Europe upon bull to left, *medium*   *s.* ·75

502 ℺ temple—℞ similar, *not good*   *s.* ·75

503 O- head of Augustus to right—℞ ΣΙΔΩΝΩΣ, Europe on
bull galloping to left, *not good*   *s.* ·9

504 O- the same—℞ similar, bull to right, same size, *not
good*   *s.* ·9

505 O- head of Claudius to right — ℞ ΣΙΔΩΝΩΣ ΝΑΥΑΡ·
ΧΙΔΟC (partly erased), male figure standing, to right,
upon prow of galley, date ΖΚΣ : *two coins, not good*
s. ·9

506 O- head of Nero with radiate crown to right — ℞
ΣΙΔΩΝΩΣ ΘΕΑΣ, Europe on bull to right, date ΖΚΣ,
very good   *s.* ·9

507 O- head of Caracalla to right, IMP. M. AVP. ANTON.
. . . .—℞ circular legend erased, table with two vases
for games, above ACTIA, below ERACLIA, *not good*
s. 1·

508 O- bust of Elagabalus to right, IM. C. M. AV. ANTO-
NINVS. AVG.,—℞ COL. AVR. PIA. MET. in ex.
SIDON., three military ensigns; *two coins, one very
good, one inferior*   *s.* 1·15

509 O- the same—℞ same inscription (partly out of coin),
Europe on bull to right, *good*   *s.* 1·05

510 O- the same—℞ same inscription, large urn for games,
above it covered chariot, *medium*   *s.* 1·05

511 O- the same—℞ same inscriptions, table supporting urn
of games, *medium*   *s.* 1·

512 O- the same—℞ same inscription, covered chariot, inside
statue of Astartea ; *two coins, one very good, one inferior*   *s.* 1·

513 O- the same—℞ similar, *very good*   *s.* ·75

514 O- head of Maesa to right —℞ COL. AVR. PIA. ME.
SIDON, Europe on bull, to right, *very good*   *s.* ·9

515 O- the same—℞ same inscription, three military ensigns,
medium   *s.* 1·

TRIPOLIS (OF SYRIA).

COPPER COINS.

516 O heads of Dioscuri to right, with crowns of laurel—℞ Victory standing on prow of galley, to left, holding crown TPIΠOΛITΩN. above galley, below L. $\frac{M\Delta}{TKE}$; *two coins, one very good, one inferior* s. ·85

517 O unadorned head of Dioscuri to r.—℞ TPIΠOΛITΩN, figure standing dressed in short tunic, right hand on sword or stick, holding in left cornucopia, *medium* s. ·75

518 O the same—℞ part of galley with Phenician letters; *two coins, good* s. ·6

519 O head of female with mural crown to right—℞ Dioscuri standing, holding horses ; in ex. inscription (TPIΠO-ΛITΩN) very much erased, *not good* s. ·8

520 O the same—℞ Dioscuri on horseback galloping to right, above same inscription, very small, erased, *medium* s. ·6

521 O the same—℞ Victory on prow of galley to right, holding crown ; *three coins, one good, two not good* s. ·7 *to* ·95

COLONIAL COINS.

COPPER.

522 O head of Nero to right (on neck quadrangular counter-mark IMP. V (Imperator Vespasianus)—℞ TPIΠO-ΛEITΩN, heads of Dioscuri with caps, to right ; *two coins, one good, one inferior* s. ·95

523 O bust of Hadrian to right, naked shoulders, AYTOKP. KAICAP TPAIANOC AΔPIANOC—℞ TPIΠOΛEI-TΩN. Astartea to left holding trident in right hand, date HKY. ; *two coins, one very good, one inferior, s.* ·95

524 O the same—℞ TPIΠOΛEITΩN, heads of Dioscuri ; with caps to right ; *two coins, medium* s. ·95

525 O the same—℞ TPIΠOΛEITΩN, Victory upon galley going to left, date IIKY, *good* s. ·8

F

526 ☉ head of Antoninus Pius, legend erased—℞ ΤΡΙΠΟ·
ΛΕΙΤΩΝ, Astartea holding trident, date ☉ Ν Υ., *not
good* s. '9

527 ☉ head of Julia Domna to right, ΔΩΜΝΑ CEBACTH—
℞ ΤΡΙΠΟΛΙΤΩΝ, temple with four columns in centre,
altar burning; on sides figures standing, below, date
ΞΚΦ, *very good* s. 1'15

528 ☉ head of Caracalla to left, ΜΑΡ. ΑΥΡ ΑΝΤΩΝΙΝΟC—
℞ ΤΡΙΠΟΛΙΤΩΝ, temple with four columns; in centre
altar burning; on left side naked male figure standing,
right arm extended; on left draped female figure,
below date ΑΛΦ, *good* s. 1'1

529 ☉ the same—℞ similar, date ΔΑΦ; *three coins, one very
good, two inferior* s. 1'

ARADUS.

Autonomous Coins in silver.

530 ☉ bust of female with mural crown to right—℞ ΑΡΑ·
ΔΙΩΝ, Victory to left, holding acrostolium in right
hand; in left palm; the whole in crown of leaves,
date ΗΙΡ (118) below $\frac{Λ}{ΕΣ}$, *medium* s. 1'05

531 ☉ the same—℞ similar, date ΞΟΡ (177), below $\frac{q}{ΘΕ}$
medium s. 1'05

532 ☉ the same—℞ similar, date ΑΟΡ (171) below $\frac{ΧΙ}{ΜΣ}$; *two
coins, fleur de coin* s. 1'1

533 ☉ the same—℞ similar, same date, below $\frac{Λ}{ΜΣ}$, *fleur de
coin* s. 1'1

534 ☉ the same—℞ similar, date ΔΠΡ (184), below $\frac{q}{ΜΣ}$
good s. '9

535 ☉ the same—℞ similar, date ΕΠΡ (185), below $\frac{Λ}{ΜΣ}$
good s. '9

536 ☉ bee with monograms to right and left—℞ ΑΡΑΔΙΩΝ,
stag and palm tree; *three coins, two fleur de coin, one
inferior* s. '75

537 ☉ male head with beard to right —℞ A. afterpart of galley with rudder, *medium*　　　　s. ·5

538 ☉ female head with mural crown to right—℞ A. afterpart of galley with rudder, *good*　　　　s. ·5

COPPER COINS.

539 ☉ veiled head of female to left—℞ bull galloping to left, above ΦΣ CN, below POΔ NΞI, *very good*　　　s. ·8

540 ☉ veiled head of female to right, before it small head of Trajan—℞ APAΔIΩN, bull running to left, above EΞT (395), good　　　s. ·8

541 ☉ head of female diademed, small head of Trajan— ℞ similar, date EOT (375), *medium*

542 ☉ heads of Marcus Aurelius and Verus, ANTΩNINOC KAI OYPOC CEBACTOI (only partly visible)—℞ APAΔIΩN, female holding cornucopia seated on rudder, date AKY (420), *good*　　　s. ·9

543 ☉ head of Elagabalus, AYT. KAI. M. AYP. ANTΩN-INOC.—℞ APAΔIΩN, Cypress; to right lion, and to left bull, two military ensigns, *not good*　　　s. 1·2

BYBLUS.

AUTONOMOUS COINS IN COPPER.

544 ☉ head of Jupiter to right—℞ legend erased, Isis Pharia to right, holding sail, *not good*　　　s. ·8

545 ☉ head of female to left—℞ similar, *not good*　　s. 9

COLONIAL COINS.

546 ☉ head of Augustus to right KAIΣAP ΣEBACTOΣ—℞ figure standing with six wings holding long sceptre, to left; BY. LA. to right, Phenician letters, *two coins, one good, one medium*　　　s. ·8

547 ☉ same head with countermark of smaller head on neck, legend erased—℞ female figure standing to right and facing smaller one to left BYBAYШN., to right I.B., *not good*　　　s. ·9

548 O bust of Marcus Aurelius to right . . . M. AVP.
ANTΩNIN. . . . —℞ . . . . BYBA . . temple with circular roof, in middle of which Astartea to right leaning
on spear, crowned by Victory on stand, *not good* s. ·9

549 O bust of Commodus to right, legend partly visible—
℞ IEPAC BYBAOY, Astartea in temple as above, *three
coins, medium* s. 1·15 *to* ·95

550 O head of Commodus to right M. AV. KOMMOΔOC . . .
℞ IEPAC BYBAOY, Isis, Pharia to left holding sail,
three coins, one very good, two good s. ·9

551 O bust of Septimus Severus to right . . . CEIITIM
COYHPOC. CEB. —℞ IEPAC BYBAOY, temple in
middle of which Astartea crowned by Victory, *good* s. 1·1

552 O bust of Macrinus to right, AYT. KAI. C. MAKPINOC.
CEB. —℞ large temple of Byblos, above IEPAC, below
BYB . . ., *medium* s. 1·2

553 O bust of Diadumenianus to right with unadorned head
and armour M, OΩ. ΔIAΔ . . . . . ANOC. KAI- (struck
partly out of coin)—℞ Astartea in temple to left BYB,
below IEPAC, to right AOY, *very good* s. ·9

554 O bust of Elagabalus to right . . M. AYP. ANTΩNINOC
—℞ same type, to left IEPAC, to right BYBAOY, *very
good* s. 1·2

555 O bust of Elagabalus to right (legend erased)—℞ same
type, above IEPAC, below BYBAOY, *medium* s. ·95

556 O the same M. AYP ANTΩNINOC.—℞ IEPAC BYBAOY,
Isis Pharia to right, holding sail, *very good* s. ·95

PHOENICE IN GENERE.

557 O legend, confused head of Diadumenianus—℞ COL.
NV. PHO. . . . . temple seen sideways (*copper*) *not
good* s. 1

COMMAGENE.

COPPER COINS.

558 O two hands clasped and caducea, above ΠIΣ, below
TIΣ—℞ KOMMAΓHNΩN, anchor, *good* s. ·6

53

GERMANICA CAESAREA.

559 G .... KOMMOΔOC .... bust of Commodus to right
—℞ KAIC. ΓEPMANIKAIΩN, female seated on rocks
to left, at her feet river swimming, *good*   *s.* ·95

SAMOSATE.

560 G AYT. K. M. AYP. AN. .... bust of Marcus Aurelius to
right—℞ Φ. CAM. IEP. ACY. E. female seated on rocks,
at her feet river swimming, *good*   *s.* ·9
561 G AYT. K. M. IOYΛ ΦΙΛΙΠΠOC. bust of Philippus
(father) to right—℞ ΦΛ. CAMOCATEΩN. MHTPOII.
KOMA., female seated on rocks to left, holds eagle in
right hand ; at her feet Pegasus running, *medium s.* 1·3
562 G same description, bust of young Philippus to right—
℞ CAMOCATEΩN, same type as above, *good*   *s.* 1·15
563 G BAΣI .... TIOXOY. head of Antiochus IV to right,
with countermark on neck of king—℞ KOMMAΓHNΩN,
scorpion in wreath, *not good*   *s.* 1

COELE SYRIA.

LAODICEA AD LIBANUM.

564 G ... MAKPINOC. CEΠ. bust of Macrinus to right —
℞ ΛAOΔIK .... figure with Phrygian cap, holding
horse by bridle   *s.* 1·1
   ⁎ Legends on both sides are much erased, but face and
   reverse of coin are good.

HELIOPOLIS.

565 G head of Septimus Severus to right (legend erased)—
℞ I. O. M. H. below COL. HEL. large temple ; *two
coins, not good*   *s.* 1·
566 G ANTONINVS ... AVG. head of Caracalla to right
—℞ COL. HEL. head of female with mural crown to
left, behind cornucopia, *medium*   *s.* ·9

567   ʘ GETA. CAESAR. head of Geta to right--℞ COL.
HEL. head of female with mural crown and veil to
left, *good*   *s.* 1.

568   ʘ IMP. CAES. M. IVL. PHILIPPVS. PIVS. FEL.
AVG. bust of Philippus to right -℞ COL. IVL. AVG.
FEL. (in ex. HEL. erased) large figure of female
holding rudder and cornucopia ; on each side two
smaller ones holding veil over her head, below two
small figures, *good*   *s.* 1·1

569   ʘ OTACILIA. SEVERA. AVG. bust of Otacillia to
right—℞ COL. IVL. AVG. FEL. I. O. M. II. large
temple facing with cypress in centre of door ; below
COL. HEL. ; *two coins, good*   *s.* 1·15

570   ʘ IMP. CAES. P. LIC. GALLIE. NVS., bust of Gallienus to right—℞ COL. AV. CER. SA...... large
urn for games ; below in two lines, CAP. OEC. ISE.
HEL. *good*   *s.* 1·1

LEUCAS.

571   ʘ AYT. KAICAP. head of emperor (Domitianus?) to
left—℞ ΛΕΥΚΑ ΚΛΑΥΔΙΕΩΝ figure in chariot, drawn
by four horses to right. *medium*   *s.* ·8

TRACHONITIS ITUREA.

PHILIPPUS TETRARCH.

572   ʘ ΣΕΒΑΣ, Head of Augustus to right — ℞ ΕΠΙ.
ΦΙΛΙΠΠΟΥ, temple in middle of which L. A., *good s.* ·7

CAESAREA.

573   ʘ CAESAR, head of Augustus to right—℞ AVGVSTVS
in crown ; *three coins, good*   *s.* 1.

574   ʘ head of Septimus Severus to right—℞ Pan playing
flute, leaning on column, *not good*

NERONIAS.

575 ℺ head of Nero to right—℞ ΕΠΙ. ΒΑΣΙ. ΑΓΡΙΠΠΑ.
ΝΕΡΩΝΙΕ, in five lines; the whole in a circle, *good*, *s.* ·6

DECAPOLE.

ABILA.

576 ℺ A. ΚΟΜΜΟΔΟC...., bust of Commodus to right—
℞ CE. ΑΒΙΛ.... ΑΓΒ. NC. (year 250), Hercules
standing to right, *good* *s.* ·9

GADARA.

577 ℺ head of Gordianus to right (legend partly erased)—℞
(Γ) ΑΔΑΡΕ. ΩΝ., galley with oarsman in ex. ΓΜ.
(year 303), *face bad, reverse good* *s.* I·

GABA.

578 ℺ ... ΚΑΙ. ΑΝΤΩΝΕΙΝΟC., head of Antoninus to right
—℞ ΓΑΒΗ-ΝΩΝ-ΖΙC. (year 217), draped figure with
Phrygian cap, facing, holds spear in right hand, *very
good* *s.* ·9

DIUM (?)

579 ℺ head of female to right—℞ ΔΚΣ. ΔΙΟΥ. Α., in three
lines, *good* *s.* ·45

SAMARITIS.

580 ℺ ... ΤΡΑ. HADRIAN..., head of Hadrian to right—
℞ COL. P. FL. AVG., colonist leading two oxen to
right is crowned by small figure of Victory, *medium*
s. I·2

581 ℺ head of Alexander Severus to right, IM. C. M. SEV.
ALEX....—℞ C. I. P. F., eagle with spread wings;
in centre S. P. Q. R. ; *two coins, not good* *s.* ·9 *and* ·7

582 O· head of Macrinus to right . . . OII. CE. MAKPINOC.
CE.—Ɗ. ΦΛ. ΝΕΑCΠΟΛΕШC. CY. ΠΑΛΕ., figure of
Rome seated to left on shield, holding Victory in right
hand, left resting on spear, *good*   *s.* 1·15

583 O· head of Elagabalus to right, AYT. KAI . . . . TONINVS.
. . .—Ɗ. ΦΛ. ΝΕΑCΠΟΛΕШC., Mount Garizim, on the
top temple, below eagle with spread wings ; *four coins,
one very good, three medium*   *s.* 1·

584 O· head of Geta, to right GETAC. AVG.—Ɗ. CEBACTII
. . . CYP., figure with helmet standing to right, right
hand resting on spear, *good*   *s.* ·9

GALILEA.

PTOLÉMAÏS.

585 O· head of Trajan to left, legend partly erased—Ɗ. COL.
PTOL., female figure seated on rocks to right, *not
good*   *s.* 1·

SEPPHORIS-DIOCAESAREA.

586 O· head of Trajan to right, legend erased—Ɗ. ΣΕΠΦΟ . . .
palm tree with fruits, *not good*   *s.* ·9

TIBERIAS.

587 O· head of Trajan to right, . . . NOC. CEB. ΓΕΡΜ . . .—
Ɗ. TIBEP. KΛΑΔI., female (Hygeia) seated to right,
at her feet spring of water flowing, *medium*   *s.* ·9

AELIA CAPITOLINA.

588 O· bust of Trajanus Decius to right, . . . TRA. DECIVS.
AVG.—Ɗ. COL. AE . . . . . OM. PF., female standing
to left, hand extended, holding indistinct object, Victory behind on stand crowning her, to left ensign
supporting eagle, *not good*   *s.* 1·1

Undetermined Coin of Palestine.

589 ℧ IM. CAES . . . DIVI. AVGVSTI. TI. F. AVG., head
of Tiberius to right—℞ PONT. MAXI. TR. POT.
XXII., two cornucopiae, in middle caducea, *good*
s. 1·15

BOSTRA.

590 ℧ IOYAIA MAMEA., bust of Mamea to right—℞ NE.
TR . . . BOC . . ., Astartea to right, in middle of
temple with four columns, *not good* *s.* 1·2

591 ℧ IVLIA. MAMEA. AVGVSTA., bust of Mamea to
right—℞ COLONIA BOSTRA., bust of female, with
mural crown to left, on her shoulder cornucopia,
medium *s.* ·9

592 ℧ IMP. CAES. M. IVL. PHILIPPOS. AVG., bust of
Phillipus to right—℞ COL. MET. BOCTRA., male
head to right, *medium* *s.* 1·1

593 ℧ ΔOMNA, bust of Domna to right—℞ NE. TRA.
BOCTRA, Astartea, in temple, *not good* *s.* 1·2

JUDEA.

(Small Copper Coins struck under the Roman
Procurators.)

AUGUSTUS (Marcus Ambivius, Procurator).

594 ℧ KAICA-POC', ear of wheat—℞ date tree with fruit hanging; date ΛΘ (39th year of Augustean era), *good s.* ·6

(Amicus Rufus, Procurator).

595 ℧ the same—℞ similar; date M A (41st year), *good s.* ·6
596 ℧ the same—℞ similar (date not visible), *good* *s.* ·6

TIBERIUS (Valerius Gratus, Procurator).

597 ℧ IOYAIA (Tiberius' mother), in crown of leaves—
℞ ear of wheat, to left L, to right B (second year of
Tiberius), *good* *s.* ·6

58

(Pontius Pilatus, Procurator).

598 ☾ TIBEPIOY KAICAPOC, Lituus—℞ IH in crown
(18th year of Tiberius, corresponding to year 32 of
Christian era, and to the epoch of prediction of our
Lord), *good*   *s.* ·6

NERO and BRITANNICUS (Claudius Felix, Procurator).

599 ☾ NEPW. KΛAV., two shields and arrows—℞ date
palm, with fruits ; above, BP IT ; below, KAI. L. IΔ
(14th year of Claudius), *good*   *s.* ·6

(Porcius Felix, Procurator).

600 ☾ L. E. KAICAPOC, palm—℞ NEP. ΩNO-C-, in three
lines in crown (5th year of Nero); *two coins, very
good*   *s.* ·6

Coins (Copper) struck by Titus and Domitian after the Fall of Jerusalem.

601 ☾ AYTOK . . . . head of Titus to right—℞ (IOYΔA)
IAΣ. EΛΔШKYI (AΣ), trophy of arms ; to left, female
kneeling ; to right, pelta (small shield), *good*   *s.* 1·

602 ☾ AYTOK. KAIΣAP., head of Titus to right—℞ IOY-
ΔAIAΣ. EAΔШKYIAΣ, Victory, with foot on helmet,
writing upon shield suspended to palm-tree (five coins
with slight variations, legends completing one another),
good   *s.* ·8

DOMITIANUS and AGRIPPA II.

603 ☾ Legend erased, head of Domitianus to right—℞ female
standing holding cornucopia; to left, $\frac{\Delta i}{A\Gamma Pi}$ to right, $\frac{DA}{\Pi\Pi A}$
                                                         s. 1·1√

604 ☾ ΔOMITIANOC . . ., head of Domitian to right—℞
ETOYC . . . . AΓPIΠΠA, Victory to right, writing on
shield, *good*   *s.* ·8

JEWISH PRINCES OR HIGH PRIESTS.

605 ℺ vase with handles, legend in Hebraic letters—℞ tree with fruits hanging, Hebraic letters (*copper*) ; *two coins, medium*   *s.* ·7

JUDAS MACHABEUS or JONATHAN (?).

606 ℺ Hebraic legend in four lines in middle of crown—℞ two cornucopiæ tied at the end ; in middle, pomegranate (*copper*) ; *two coins, very good*   *s.* ·6

HERODES ARCHÉLAUS.

607 ℺ (IIPO)ΔOY, vine leaf—℞ EΘNAPXOY (very indistinct), helmet (*copper*), *medium*   *s.* ·6

AGRIPPA I.

608 ℺ ΒΑΣΙΛΕΩΣΑΓΡΙΠΠΑ, parasol with fringe—℞ three ears of wheat, L Σ (year 6), (*copper*); *four coins, good*   *s.* ·7

(SMALL COPPER COINS, STRUCK IN JUDEA, WITH PORTRAIT, *not determined.*

609 ℺ head of Emperor to right—TIBEP (K)ΛAY in middle (anchor), *good*   *s.* ·6
610 ℺ head to right—℞ palm, A C, *not good*   *s.* ·6
611 ℺ head of Emperor or King to right—℞ palm tree with fruit ; to left, N ; to right, P, *good*   *s.* ·6
612 ℺ head of Emperor (Titus or Domitian?) to right- -℞ lotus flower, L Z, *good*   *s.* ·6
613 ℺ the same—℞ similar, but size 4, *good*   *o.* ·4

ASCALON.

614 ℺ head of female with mural crown—℞ A Σ, prow of galley ; *three coins, good*   *s.* ·5
615 ℺ CEBACTOC, head of Augustus to right—℞ AΣKAAΩ, female figure facing, holding spear in right hand, *not good*   *s.* 1·
616 ℺ head of Domitian—℞ similar to right, of female, dove, and date Δ II P, *not good*   *s.* ·9

GAZA.

617 O· head of Antoninus Pius to right, ANTWNINOC—℞
ΓΑΖΑ ΕΙC (215), female figure, draped, holding spear
in right hand and cornucopia ; to left, cow (I O), (year
215 of Gaza = 154 A. D.), *good*   s. ·9

618 O· head of Julia Domna to right, ΔOMNA—℞ ΓΑΖΑ·ΕΙW,
two females facing each other, holding hands (genius
of town and I O) ; in ex. S Ξ C (year 266 of Gaza =
195 A. D.), *good*   s. ·7

619 O· AYT.K.M.A. ANTΩNEINOC, head of Elagabalus to
to right—℞ ΓΑΖΑ·WNE.ΠC, draped female to left, holding crown in right hand ; before her bird, *good* s. ɪ·ɪ√

SELEUCIS PIERIA.

APAMEA.

620 O· head of Jupiter to right—℞ AΠAMEΩN. TΩΣ.
IEPAΣ. KAI. AΣIΛOY., elephant to right, before
elephant I ; *two coins, one good, one medium*   s. ·8

BALANEA.

621 O· head of Augustus to right—℞ BAΛΛΝΕ . . ., figure in
helmet, in chariot drawn by four horses to left, above
N. behind ΞO., *not good*   s. ·9

EMISA.

622 O· . . . . TΩNI. NOC. CEB. head of Caracalla to right—
℞ . . . MICΩN. KOΛΩNIAC., temple with six columns,
with rough figure in middle, *not good*   s. ɪ·2

GABALA.

623 O· AYT. K. M. A. ANTΩNINOC., head of Caracalla to
right—℞ . . . BAΛΕΩN. female figure sitting to left
with cornucopia, *not good*   s. ɪ·ɪ

LAODICEA.

624 O head of Bacchus to left —℞ ΛΑΟΔΙΚΕΩΝ., female figure to left holding object in extended hand, *very good*
s. '7

625 O head of female with mural crown to right and veil— ΙΟΥΛΙΕΩΝ. ΤΩΝ. ΚΑΙ. ΛΑΟΔΙΚΕΩΝ., winged Victory to left holding crown, *very good*
s. '7

626 O the same—℞ same legend, female standing to left with cornucopia, *good*
s. '9

627 O head of Bacchus to right—℞ ΛΑΟΔΙΚΕΩΝ. Victory to left, *very good*
s. '5

628 O head of Pallas without helmet—℞ ΙΟΥΛΙΕΩΝ. ΤΩΝ. ΚΑΙ. ΛΑΟΔΙΚΕΩΝ. owl ; *three coins, good*
s. '5

629 O ... ΚΛΑΥΔΙΟΥ. ΚΑΙCΑΡ. head of Claudius to right —℞ same legend as above, female standing and facing, with cornucopia, *good*
s. '9

630 O ΑΥΤΟΚΡ. ΝΕΡ. ΤΡΑΙΑΝΟC. ΑΡΙCΤ. ΚΑΙC. ΓΕΡ. ΔΑC. head of Trajan to right—℞ same legend, head of female to right with mural crown and veil, *very good*
s. 1'1

631 O head of emperor to left (no legend)—℞ similar, *medium*
s. 1'

632 O ΑΥΤΟΚ. ΚΑΙ. ΔΟΜΙΤΙΑΝΟΥ. ΓΕΡΜΑΝΙΚΟΥ., head of Domitian—℞ same legend, Fortuna holding crown and cornucopia to left ; *two coins, good*
s. '8

ANTONINUS.

633 O ΑΥΤΟΚ. ΚΑΙ. ΑΝΤ... head to right—℞ ΛΑ........ ΛΙΤΩΝ. female standing to right holds small figure in left hand, right hand on rudder, *medium*
s. 1'

634 O ... ΑVR. ANTONINUS, head of Caracalla to right —℞ ROMAE. FEL., Romulus and Remus sucking wolf, *not good*
s. 1'1

635 O ΑΥΤΟΚ. Κ. ΙΟΥΛ. ΦΙΛΙΙΙΙΟC. CΕΒ. head of Philippus to right—℞ COL. LAOD. METROPOLEOS., female seated, facing, and four other figures around her in ex. CE., *very good*
s. 1'

636 O .... ANTON ..... head of Elagabalus to right
R COL LAOD. ..... draped figure of female seated
to left, before her young male figure standing with
right arm uplifted; between them star and crescent,
*legends on both sides partly struck out of coin, otherwise
very good*   s. 1·1 √

SELEUCIA.

637 O head of female with mural crown to right or left——
R CEΛEYKEΩN. THC. IEPAC. KAI. AYTONOMOY.
thunderbolt on table (*copper*), *four coins, two very good,
two medium*   s. ·8

638 O AYTOKP. KAIC. NEP. TPAIANOC. head of Trajan
to right — R CEΛEYKEΩN. ΠIEPAC. below Z.
KACIOC. temple in middle of which conical stone
(barbarous) *medium*   s. 1·

639 O ... CEYEPOC. head of Septimus Severus to right—
R CEΛEYΩ. thunderbolt on table, *not good*   s. ·9

640 O ... MA. ANTΩNEIN .... Elagabalus to right—R
CEΛEYKEΩN, temple with conical stone in middle,
and eagle at the top, *good*   s. 1·5

641 O AYT. KAI. MAP. AYP. CE. AΛEΞAN. ΔPOC. C. bust
of Alexandrus Severus to right—R CEΛEYKEΩN.
ΠIEPAC. below OΘB. same type as above, *good* s. 1·2

ZEUGMA.

642 O ZEYPMATEΩN. head of female to right, in wreath—
R large Z in wreath, *barbarous, but good*   s. ·8√

643 O .AYT. KAI....... NINOC., bust of Marcus Aurelius to
left—R ZEYPMATEΩN., temple on summit of high
mountain, *not good*   s. ·9

644 O .... TONINOC., bust of Antoninus Pius to right—
R similar, temple on mountain in wreath, *good* s. ·9

645 O AYTOK. K. IOYAI. ΦIΛIΠΠOC. CEB., bust of young
Philippus to right—R ZEYPMATEΩN., temple on
summit of mountain, *good*   s. 1·1√

646 O MAP. OTAKIA. CEOYHPAN. CEB., bust of Otacilla
to right—R similar, *very good*   s. 1·1 √

CYRRHESTICA.

BEROA (ALEP.)

647 ℺ head of Trajan to right—℞ BEPOIΑΩΝ., in ex. I, the whole in wreath, *medium*   *s.* ·9

CYRRHUS.

648 ℺ ...TOP. KAIC. AP. TITO. AIΛ. ΑΝΤΩΝΙΝΟC., head of Antoninus to right—℞ ΔΙΟC. ΚΑΤΑΙΒΑΤΟΥ. ΚΥΡΡΗCΤΩΝ., Jupiter seated to left, holding thunderbolt ; at his feet, eagle ; behind D ; *two coins—one very good, one inferior*   *s.* ·9

649 ℺ ...KOMMO...., head of Commodus to right—℞ .... ΒΑΤΟΥ. ΚΥΡΡΗC... similar, behind Jupiter Γ, *medium*   *s.* ·9

HIEROPOLIS.

650 ℺ .... ΑΔΡΙ. ΑΝΤΩΝΕΙΝΟC., bust of Antoninus Pius to right—℞ ΘΕΑC. CΥΡΙΑC. ΙΕΡΟΠΟΛ. in wreath, *medium*   *s.* ·9√

651 ℺ ΑΥΤ......... ΛΟΥ. (legend nearly all out of coin), head of Marcus Aurelius to right—℞ similar, below Z, *very good*   *s.* ·8√

652 ℺ ΑΥΤ. K. M. ΑΥΡ. ΑΝΤ....., bust of Marcus Aurelius to right—℞ CΥΡΙΑC. ΙΕΡΟΠΟΛΙΤΩΝ, Cybele upon lion going to left, *medium*   *s.* 1·3

653 ℺ ΑΥΤΟΚ. K. M. ΙΟΥΛΙ. ΦΙΛΙΠΠΟC. CΕΒ., bust of Philippus to right—℞ ΘΕΑC. CΥΡΙΑC. ΙΕΡΟΠΟ-ΛΙΤΩΝ., Cybele on lion going to right, *good*

MESOPOTAMIA.

EDESSA.

654 ℺ ....ΑΝΤΩΝΕΙΝΟC....., bust of Caracalla to left—℞ ΚΟΛ. ΜΑΡ. ΕΔΕ...., head of female with mural crown to left, *medium*   *s.* ·65

655 O .. KAI. M. AYP. ANTΩNE...., bust of Elagabalus to
left—℞ similar, *medium*   *s.* ·65

656 O AYTO. KAI. MAP. AYP. ANTΩNE., bust of Elagabalus to left—℞ KOAΩ. MAP. EΔECCA., female
seated on rocks to left, *very good*   *s.* 1·°5

657 O AYT. KAI. M. AY. CE. AΛEΞANAPOC., bust of
Alexandrus Severus to right—℞ M HT. KOΛ. EΔEC-
CHΩN., female as above ; before her, altar ; right and
left two stars, *very good*   *s.* 1·

658 O ....AΛEΞANΔPOC...., head of Emperor with beard
to left—℞ similar, *good*   *s.* 1·

KINGS OF EDESSE.

659 O ....PATOP. CEOYHPOC., head of Septimus Severus
to right—℞ UACIΛEYC. ABΓAPOC., head of King
with tiara, *good*

660 O AYTOKPATOP......, head of Gordian III to right,
before star—℞ BACIEYC...., head of King to right,
with tiara ; behind, star, *medium*

MAIOZAMALCHA.

661 O bust of Emperor radiate to right (*legend barbarous*),
ENOYTIΛM EKYVINTY VMC (*sic*) — ℞ MAIO.
COLONIA., female seated to left, with mural crown ;
to right and left two ensigns, with s. c. ; below, two
male figures swimming, *very good*   *s.* 1·3

NISIBI.

662 O .....ΞANΔPOC., head of Alexander Severus to right—
℞ ....KOΛ. NECIBI. MHT., head of female with
mural crown to right ; before and behind, stars ; above,
ram running to right, *two coins—good*   *s.* 1·1

663 O .AYTOK. K. M. IOYΛI. ΦIΛIΠΠOC. CEB., bust of
Philippus to right—℞ IOYΛ. CEΠ. KOΛΩ. NECIBI.,
female figure, facing, in temple, *very good*   *s.* 1·

RHESAENA.

664 O . . . MEKY. TPAIANOC . ΔEKIOC . CEB., bust of Decius to right — ℞. CEB . KOΛ . PHCAINHCIΩN . L .
I I I . ., two female figures with hands clasped ; above,
eagle, *good*   *s.* 1·05

665 O same inscription and head—℞ same inscription, and
Colonist leading two oxen to right ; above, eagle,
medium   *s.* 1·0

SINGARA.

666 O AYTOK. K. M. ANT. ΓOPΔIANOC. CEB., bust of
Gordianus III to right—℞ AYP.CEII.KOΛ. CINΓAPA.,
head of female, with mural crown and veil to right,
above Sagittarius ; *two coins, very good*   *s.* 1·5

667 O AYTOK. K. M. ANT. ΓOPΔIANOC. CAB. TPAN-
KYΛΛI. NΔ. CEB., heads of Gordianus and Tranquil-
lina facing—℞ AYP. CEII. KOΛ. CINΓAPA., female
seated on rocks to left, above Sagittarius to left, *very
good*   *s.* 1·2

ASSYRIA.

CLAUDIOPOLIS (NINIVA).

668 O IMP. C. S. IVLVS. MAXIMINVS., bust of Maxi-
minus to right—℞ upper part of legend out of coin,
in ex. CLAV., colonist leading two oxen to right,
above military ensign, *very good*   *s.* 1·1

CILICIA,

AND VARIOUS CITIES OF ASIA MINOR.

ANAZARBUS.

669 O AYT. M. KOMOΔOC., bust of Commodus to right—
℞ ANAZAPBOY., head of female, with mural crown
and veil to right (*copper*), *good*   *s.* ·85

F

670 O AYT. K. P. ΛIK. OYΛΛEPIANOC. CEB., bust of
Valerianus to right—℞ ANAZAPBOY., two figures
seated on chairs to left, one behind the other (copper),
medium   s. 1·1

671 O the same — ℞ ANAZAPBOY., Bacchus seated on
panther running to right, in ex. ET. BOC. A.M.K.,
(copper), very good   s. 1·05

672 O the same—O six urns for games, in two rows, above
MHTPOΠ., in middle ET. BOC., below ANAZAP
BOY
(copper), medium   s. 1·2

673 O AYTK. OYΛΛEPIANOC., bust of Valerianus to right
—℞ ANAZAPBOY. MHTP. ET. BOC., male figure to
right, to right $\frac{A}{H}$ to left $\frac{T}{\Gamma}$ (copper), medium   s. 1·

674 O EPENNIA. ETP . . . ., bust of Etruscilla on crescent
to right—℞ ANAZAPBOY., Bacchus on panther to
right (copper), good   s. 1·1

675 O . . TO. OYCT. KYINTOC. CEB., bust of Hostilianus
to right—℞ ANAZAPBOY (confused), veiled head of
female to right (copper), not good   s. ·9

ANEMURIUM.

676 O AYT. K . . . . (rest of legend out of coin), bust of
Emperor, radiate, to right, with armour—℞ ET. A.
ANEMOYPIEΩN., naked male figure facing, with head
to right, holding sword in right hand, and large head
in left (copper), good   s. 1·2

ADANA.

677 O bust of Pallas to right, with helmet and armour—℞
Victory holding wreath, to left AΔANEΩN. (copper),
medium   s. ·9

678 O bust of Valerianus to right (legend partly erased)—
℞ AΔPIANΩN AΔANEΩN, Jupiter seated to left, left
hand leaning on spear (copper), medium,   s. 1·2

CELENDERIS.

679 ○ head of female, with mural crown and veil to right behind ΑΣ., the whole in circle of dots—℞ .. ΑΕΝΔΕ-ΡΙΤΩΝ., Apollo naked, leaning on cippus, holding branch of olive in right hand, above F (*copper*), *very good*   *s.* ·85

COLYBRASSUS.

680 ○ ΑΥΤ. Κ ..... ΑΝΤΩΝΙΝΟC., head of Marcus Aurelius to left—℞ ΚΟΛΥΒΡΑC ..., male figure, with toga facing, to right high tower (*copper*), *medium*   *s.* 1·

HIEROPOLIS.

681 ○ bust of Commodus to right (legend erased)—℞ ΙΕΡΟΠΟΛΕΙΤΩΝ. ΤΩΝ. ΠΡΟC. ΠΥΡΑΜΟΥ., Emperor in armour to left, receiving crown from Province facing him (*copper*), *face not good, reverse medium*   *s.* 1·5

IRENOPOLIS.

682 ○ bust of Emperor to right (legend confused)—℞ ΙΡΗΝΟΠΟΛ ....., Warrior on horseback to left, holding sword in right hand (*copper*), *medium*   *s.* 1·

MOPSUS.

683 ○ head of Jupiter to right, in border of dots—℞ ΜΟΨΕΑΤΩΝ., tripod for sacrifices, to left monogram, to right monogram (*copper*), *very good*   *s.* ·8

OLBA.

684 ○ ΣΕΒΑΣΤΟΣ ΣΕΒΑΣΤΟΥ ΚΑΙCΑΡ., head of Augustus to right, with crown of laurels—℞ ΑΡΧΙΕΡΕΩΣ ΑΙΑΝΤΟΣ ΤΕΥΚΡΟΥ ΤΟΠΑΡΧΟΥ, in five lines, in middle, thunderbolt (*copper*) ; *two coins, very good s.* ·95

685 ○ ΑΙΑΝΤΟΣ ΤΕΥΚΡΟΥ, head of Ajax (high priest) with round cap, to right—℞ (ΑΡ)ΧΙΕΡ (ΕΩΣ)ΤΟΠ-ΑΡΧΟΥ. ΚΕΝΝΑΤ. ΛΑΛΑΣΣ, in four lines, in middle, triquetra (*copper*), *good*

SELEUCIA AD CALICADNUM.

686 O ΑΝΤΩΝΙΟC ΓΟΡΔΙΑΝΟC, bust of Gordianus to right
—℞ CEΛEYK—EΩN. ΤΩ. ΠΡΟC. ΚΑΛΥΚΑΝΔ, two
Victories holding on table wreath, in middle of which,
ΕΛΕΥΘΕΡΑC. (*copper*), *good* *s.* 1·3

687 O ΙΟΥΛΙΑ. ΜΑΜ. . . . head of Mamea to right—℞
CEΛEYKEΩN.ΤΩΝ.ΠΡΟC.ΚΑΛΥΚΑΔΝΩ. Fortuna to
left, holding cornucopia (*mixed silver*), *not good* *s.* ·9

TARSUS.

688 O Female seated on rocks to right, holding palm; at
her feet, river swimming—℞ ΤΑΡΣΕΩΝ, Jupiter seated
to left, holding Victory; below, monogram (*copper*),
good *s.* 1·1

689 O head of Female with mural crown and veil, to right—
℞ . . . ΡΣΕΩΝ. monument known as tomb of Sardan-
apalus, three monograms, ⊠ (*copper*), *good* *s.* ·85

690 O same head—℞ ΤΑΡΣΕΩΝ. figure standing on quad-
ruped to right ; behind $\frac{CAN}{ΦΙΛΙ}$ (*copper*), *good* *s.* ·8

691 O ΤΑΡΣΕΩΝ. Jupiter seated to left and holding Victory
—℞ club in wreath, ΗΟ and ΤΠΟ—? (*copper*), *good*
s. ·6

692 O ΑΔΡΙΑΝΗC ΤΑΡΣΕΩΝ. head of Hercules to right,
with club on shoulder—℞ ΜΗΤΡΟΠΟΛΕΩC. naked
figure to left, holding fortune and harpa ; below, figure
swimming; before, $\frac{ΒΟΗ}{ΘΟΥ}$ (*copper*), *good* *s.* 1·1

693 O ΑΥΤ. ΚΑΙ. ΤΙ. ΑΙ. ΑΔΡ. ΑΝΤΩΝΗΙΝΟC. CEB. EV.
bust of Antoninus Pius to right ; before Γ. behind Π.
℞ ΑΔΡΙΑΝΩΝ. ΤΑΡCEΩΝ. . ΜΗΤΡΟΠΟΛΕ. temple
with ten columns ; on the front ΚΟΙΝΟC. ΚΙΛΙΚΙΑC.
(*copper*), *very good* *s.* 1·25

694 O . . . ΚΑΙ. Α. CEΠ. . . . . bust of Septimus Severus to
right—℞ . . . . ΥΗΡΑΝ. ΤΑΡCΟΥ, figure seated ;
behind, figure crowning her ; before, two other figures
holding crowns ; above central figure, ΚΙΛΙΚΙΑC ;
below, ΙCΑΥΡΙΑ and ΛΥΚΛΟΝΙΑ, and river swim-
ming (*copper*), *circular legend erased, other parts of coin
good* *s.* 1·5

695 G AYT. KAI. AVP. CEOYEPOC. ANTΩNEINOC. CEB., bust of Caracalla to right, with crown— ℞ ΠΑΛΛΑC. AΘHNII. TAPCEΩN., figure of Pallas to right, holding Victory in left hand, right leaning on spear (*mixture of silver and copper*), *very good*   *s.* ·8

696 G IOYAIA. MAECA . . . . ., bust of Maesa to right— ℞ TAPCOY. THΣ. MHTPOΠO., male and female figures, draped, holding each other by the hand (*copper*), *medium*   *s.* 1·2

697 G AYT. K. M. ANT. ΓOPΔIANOC. CEB., bust of Gordianus III, with armour, to right Π. Π.—℞ TAPCOY. MHTPOΠOΛEΩC., naked male figure, facing, holding bow and arrow, A. M. K. Γ. Δ.; *two coins* (*copper*), *good*   *s.* 1·35

698 G AYT. KAI. IOYΛ. ΦIΛIΠΠO. NEYTEYC. CEB., bust of Philippus to right, Π. Π. — ℞ TAPCOY. THΣ. MHTP . . ., male and female figures facing each other (*copper*), *good*   *s.* 1·4

699 G AY. KE. Γ. OYI. AΦE . . . . . CIANOC., bust of Volusianus to right — ℞ TAPCOY. MHTPOΠOΛEΩC., Victory walking to right, Γ. Λ. M. B. K. (*copper*), *good*   *s.* 1·2

700 G AY. KAI. Π. Λ. OYΛEPIANOC., bust of Valerianus to right—℞ TAPCOY. MHT . . . . ., three naked figures, facing, in ex. A. M. K. (*copper*), *medium*   *s.* 1·1

701 G same head and legend—℞ TAPCOY. MHTPOΠO. . . . ., naked figure to left, holding Fortune in right hand, A. B. Π. Γ. (*copper*), *medium*   *s.* 1·3

ZEPHYRIUM.

702 G head of female, with mural crown to right—℞ ΣEΦY-PIΩTΩN, female seated to left (*copper*), *good*   *s.* ·8

ELAEVSA.

703 G head of Jupiter to right, behind AP.- ℞ EΛΛIOYΣIΩN, Victory to right, holding crown (*copper*), *good*   *s.* ·85

CYPRUS.

704 O TI. CLAVDIVS. CAE. ... head of Claudius to left
—℞. KOINΩN. KYΠPIΩN., in three lines in crown of
laurel (*copper*), *not good*   s. 1·15

705 O AYTOKP. KAIC. NEP. TPAIANΩ. APICTΩ. CEB.
ΓEPM. ΔAC., bust of Trajan to right—℞. (ΔHMAPX
E)ẞ YΠATOC., in ex. KOINON KYΠPIΩN., Jupiter
facing (*copper*), *face very good, reverse medium*   s. 1·4

BITHYNIA.

HERACLEA.

706 O MAP. ΓOPΔIANOC. AVG., bust of Gordianus III
to right—℞. HPAKΛ ..... AΠOIKON. ΠOΛIΩN.,
naked figure of Hercules seated on rocks to left, right
hand extended, before him small figure kneeling,
carrying club, large tree (*copper*), *good*   s. 1·4

NICAEA.

707 O M. AYP. CEYH. AΛEΞANΔPOC. AYΓ., bust of
Alexander Severus to right— ℞. NIKAIEΩN., Pallas to
right, holding spear (*copper*), *not good*   s. 1·

708 O M. AYP. OYHPOC...., head of Verus to left—℞.
ΔIA. KEPCYA. NEIKAIEΩN., Jupiter standing to left
(*copper*), *good*   s. 1·

NICOMEDIA.

709 O ... AYT. OYAΛEPIANOC. ΓAΛΛHNOC ...., heads
of Valerianus and Gallienus facing each other, below
smaller head of Valerianus II—℞. NIKOMHΔEΩN.
TPEC. NEΩKOPΩN., three temples, with figure in
middle of upper one, between lower ones cistra, *good*
                                                          s. 1·1

PRUSA AD OLYMPUM.

710 O NEP. TPAIANOC. KAI. CEB. ΓEP. ΔAC., bust of
Trajan to right—℞. ΠPOYCAEΩN., female figure
standing to left, holds branch in right hand, left leans
on spear (*copper*), *good*   s. 1·3

711 Ϲ ΑV. ΝΕΡ. ΤΡΑΙΑΝΟϹ. C. K. Γ. Δ., bust of Trajan
to right—℞ ΠΡΟΥϹΑΕΩΝ., male figure, half draped,
resting in a kind of hammock, around foliage (*copper*),
very good *s.* ·9S

CAPPADOCIA.

712 Ο ΝΕRΟ. CLAVD. DI. CLAVD. F. CAESAR. AVG.
CERMA.,head of Nero to right—℞ DIVOS. CLAVD.
AVGVST. CERMANIC. PATER. AVG., head of
Claudius to right (*silver*), *very good* ˢ· *s.* ·8 ✓

CAESAREA.

713 Ϲ ΑΥΤΟΚΡ. ΚΑΙ. ΝΕΡ. ΤΡΑΙΑΝΟϹ. ϹΕΒ. ΓΕΡΜΑΝ.,
bust of Trajan to right —℞ ΔΗΜΑΡΧ. ΕΞ. ΥΠΑΤΟ...,
temple with figure in centre (*silver*), *good* *s.* ·9

714 Ϲ the same—℞ similar inscription, draped figure to left,
at her feet camel (year C), (*silver*), *good* *s.* ·9

715 Ϲ the same —℞ similar inscription, bust of elderly man,
with long beard and mural crown (year E), (*silver*) *s.* ·9

716 Ϲ the same—℞ similar inscription, bust of female to
left (year C), (*silver*), *good* *s.* ·8

717 Ϲ ΙΟΥΛΑ. Μ. ... ϹΑ., bust of Maesa to right—℞ ....
ΚΑΙϹΑΡΙ., mountain, in ex. ET. ΒΙ. (*copper*), *medium*
s. ΓΙ

718 Ϲ ΑΝΤΩΝΕΙ...., bust of Elagabalus to right— ℞ ....
ΜΗΤΡΟΠΟ. ΚΑΙϹΑ., mountain upon altar, in ex. ET. Β.
(*copper*), *medium* *s.* ΓΙ

719 Ϲ ΑΥΤ. ΚΑΙ. Μ. ΑΝΤ. ΓΟΡΔΙΑΝΟϹ. ϹΕ., bust of
Gordianus III to right—℞ .... ΚΑΙϹΑΡΙΑϹ., mountain, in ex. ΕΤΟΥϹ. C., *mixture of silver and copper*,
medium *s.* Γ

720 Ϲ ΑΥ. ΚΑ.... ΙΑΝΟϹ., bust of Gordianus III to right—
℞ ΜΗΤΡΟΠ....., mountain upon altar, ΕΝΤΙ. (*copper*), *medium* *s.* Γ

721 Ο ΑΥ. ΚΑΙ. Μ. ΑΝΤ. ΓΟΡΔΙΑΝΟϹ., bust of Gordianus
to right—℞ ΜΗΤΡ. ΚΑΙϹ. ΝΕ. ΕΤ. Ζ., basket with
ears of wheat (*copper*), *very good* *s.* ·9

CARIA.

APHRODISIAS.

722   Ꙩ IEPA. CYNKΛIITOC., head to right— ℞ ΛΦΡΟΔΙ-
CIEΩN., three branches of coral in basket (*copper*),
medium   s. 1·1

STRATONICEA.

723   Ꙩ ΛYT. KAI. ΛOY. CEΠ. CEOYHPOC...... ΔΟΜΝΑ.,
(very indistinct), busts of Septimus Severus, and
Domna facing, between them small head in counter
mask— ℞ EΠI........ CTPATONIKEΩN (very indistinct), draped figure standing to left, at her feet, altar
burning (*copper*), *legends much erased, but figures good*
         s. 1·35

IONIA.

MILETUS.

724   Ꙩ head of Apollo facing— ℞ lion to right, looking at
star behind him, ΛPΓINOΣ (*copper*), *very good*   s. ·4√

HERACLEA.

725   Ꙩ head of Hercules to right— ℞ HPΛKΛ.... Diana of
Ephesus facing (*copper*), *medium*   s. ·75

PERGA, OF PAMPHYLIA.

726   Ꙩ ΛYT. KAI. ΓΑΛΛIHNO. CEB., bust of Gallienus to
right— ℞ HEPΓAIΩN., Victory going to left (*copper*),
not good   s. 1·1

SIDE, OF PAMPHYLIA.

727   Ꙩ KOPNHΛIA KAΛΩNEINA. CEB., bust of Salonina
to right, before small countermark— ℞ CIΔIITΩN
NEΩKOPΩN., temple with four columns and high roof
inside, statue, *good*   s. 1·35

PHRYGIA.

APAMEA.

728 ℺ bust of Pallas to right—℞ ΑΠΑΜΕΩΝ., eagle with spread wings ; above, and on sides, three stars, under windings of river Meander, and caps of Dioscuri, in ex. ... HAPONIK ... (*copper*), *very good*   *s.* '9

729 ℺ the same—℞ similar, in ex. ΦΑΙΝΙΠΠΟΥ ΑΡΑΚΟΝ-ΤΟΣ (*copper*), *good*   *s.* '9

COTIAEUM.

730 ℺ ... M. ΟΤΑΚΙΛΙΑ. CΕΟΥΗΡΑ. bust of Otacilla to right—℞ ΕΠΙ. ΓΙΟΥΑΠΟΝΤΙΚΟΥ. ΑΡΧΙΕΡΕΟΣ, in ex. ΚΟΤΙΛΕΩΝ, elk kneeling with man over him (*copper*), *good*   *s.* 1·

731 ℺ ΑΥΤ. Π. ΓΑΛΛΙΗΝΟΝ, bust of Gallienus to right—℞ ΕΠΙ. ΔΗΜΗΡΙΑΝΟΥ ΙΠΠΙ ΑΡΧ. (inside) ΚΟΤΙ-ΑΕΩΝ. female facing, holding cornucopia (*copper*), *very good*   *s.* '9

SYNNADA.

732 ℺ ΒΟΥΛΗ. veiled head of female to right—℞ CΥΝΝΑ-ΔΕΩΝ. female to left, holding cornucopia (*copper*), *medium*   *s.* 1·05

ANTIOCHIA of PISIDIA.

733 ℺ IMP. C. MAR. AVR. ANT. bust of Caracalla to right—℞ ANTIOCH. FORTVNAC. female figure to left, holding cornucopia in right hand, and branch of foliage in left (*copper*), *good*   *s.* '9

734 ℺ IVLIA. AVGVSTA. bust of Julia Domna to right—℞ COL. CAES. ANTIOCH. Lunus standing to right, holding Victory and spear; to left S., to right R., at his feet bird (*copper*), *good*   *s.* 1·3

735 O IMP. M. IVL. PHILIPPVS. P. F. AVG. P. M., bust
of Philippus to right—℞ COL. CAES. ANTIOCH.
three military ensigns, between them S. R.; *two coins*
(*copper*), *good*   *s.* 1·1

AMISVS (Pontvs.)

736 O head of Dionysios to right—℞ AMIΣ. . . . Cyste of
Bacchus (*copper*), *good*   *s.* ·8

COMANA.

737 O shield of Minerva, with head of Medusa in centre—
℞ (KOMA) NΩN., Victory to right, with palm over
shoulder (*copper*), *medium*   *s.* ·8

PHARNACIA.

738 O head of Jupiter to right—℞ ΦΑΡΝΑΚΕ. . . . eagle on
thunderbolt to right; before it, monogram (*copper*),
very good   *s.* ·8

ALEXANDRIA TROAS.

739 O bust of Elagabalus to right—℞ COL. AVG. TROA.
Apollo to right, upon pedestal holding wreath (*copper*),
medium   *s.* ·8

EUROPEAN PROVINCES.

TEGEA (of Arcadia).

740 O head of Pallas to right—℞ ΤΕΓΕΑ. warrior with drawn
sword and shield to right, *copper, good*   *s.* ·8
741 O head of Apollo to right—℞ ΤΕΓΕΑ. female to right,
before her little girl presenting vase, *copper, good* *s.* ·75

PHIALEA.

742 O ANTONINVS. bust of Elagabalus to right—℞ ΦΙΑΟ-
ΛΕΩΝ., female standing to left, right hand holding
crown, left resting on spear, *copper, good*   *s.* ·85

TRAJANOPOLIS (of Thracia).

743 Ꙩ AYT. M. AYPIIAI. ANTΩNEINOC. bust of Caracalla
to right—℞ AYΓOYCTHC. TPAIANHC. naked male
figure to left holding branch of foliage in right hand,
copper, very good s. 1·2

MARCIANOPOLIS (of Moesia).

744 Ꙩ AYT. K. M. AYP. ANTΩNEINOC. AYT. IOYΛIA.
MAICA. AYT. heads of Elagabalus and Maesa facing—
℞ Y' Π IOYA. ANT. CEΛEYKOY. MAPKIANOIIO-
ΛITΩN. draped female facing to left feeding snake,
copper, medium s. 1·15

THESSALONICA (of Macedonia).

745 Ꙩ .... CEOYHP. . . . . bust of Septimus
Severus to right — ℞ ΘECCAΛONIKEΩN. Victory
going to left, *copper, medium* s. 1·1

746 Ꙩ AY. M. AV. CE. AΛEΞANP. Alexander Severus to
right—℞ same legend, draped female going to left,
at her feet altar, *copper, medium* s. 1·05√

747 Ꙩ AY. K. M. ANTO. ΓOPΔIANOC. bust of Gordianus
to right — ℞ same legend, tripod with five balls,
good s. 1·

CORCYRA.

748 Ꙩ A. KA. CEB. EPOC. ΠE. bust of Septimus Severus to
right — ℞ KOPKYPAION. Pegasus flying to right,
copper, good s. 1·

CAESAR AUGUSTA (of Spain, Saragossa).

749 Ꙩ TI. CAESAR. DIVI. AVGVSTI. F. AVGVSTVS.
head of Tiberius to left—℞ C. CA. M. CATO (L
VETT—IACVS. II. VIR. Colonist leading two oxen
to left, *copper, good* s. 1·15

FINIS.

DRYDEN PRESS :

J. DAVY AND SONS, 137, LONG ACRE, LONDON, W.C.